THE CHURCH AND THE POPE: THE CASE FOR ORTHODOXY

St. Peter the Apostle

Icon of Saint Peter, St. Catherine's Monastery, Sinai

The Church and the Pope:
The Case for Orthodoxy

by Robert B. Spencer

Uncut Mountain Press

THE CHURCH AND THE POPE
The Case for Orthodoxy

uncutmountainpress.com

Front Cover Artwork: Detail, from the Monastery of St. Catherine's Monastery on Sinai, Egypt. 5th – 6th century.

Scriptural quotations are primarily taken from the King James Version.

Library of Congress Cataloging-in-Publication Data
Robert B. Spencer, 1962 –

The Church and the Pope: The Case for Orthodoxy.—1st ed.

ISBN: 978-1-63941-005-7

I. Christian History - Eastern Orthodox
II. Christian Theology - Eastern Orthodox

Whoever calls himself universal bishop, or desires this title, is, by his pride,
the precursor to the Antichrist. — St. Gregory the Dialogist, Pope of Rome

The Church is settled on the bishops, and every act of the Church
is regulated by these same prelates. — St. Cyprian of Carthage

In the name of the Father, the Son, and the Holy Spirit.

I pray God blesses this work to be spiritually beneficial
in the journeys of Christians and non-Christians alike
who earnestly desire to know the Truth.

May He grant you courage, wisdom, and peace.

Both now and ever and unto the ages of ages. Amen.

TABLE OF CONTENTS

Christ Pantocrator

PREFACE: A PERSONAL NOTE

In 2015, after nearly thirty years as a member of the Melkite Greek Catholic Church, an Eastern Church in communion with the Roman Catholic Church, I left Roman Catholicism and shortly thereafter rejoined the Orthodox Church, the Church into which I had been baptized many years before.

My return to Orthodoxy was the result of a series of circumstances that led me to undertake a reexamination of long-held and largely unexamined premises. That reexamination ultimately led me to a rediscovery of the Orthodox Church, which in one way I never fully left. As a Melkite Greek Catholic, I had been able to participate in the Divine Liturgy of Saint John Chrysostom, the Divine Liturgy of Saint Basil the Great, and other elements of the majestic and profound Byzantine liturgical tradition.

Rediscovering and rejoining the Orthodox Church has been a great blessing to me, blessings that have aided me through difficult times.

However, this change bewildered some of my family and friends. I have been warned about hellfire. I have received numerous emails explaining to me why the true church founded by our Lord Jesus Christ was only to be found in the communion of the Bishop of Rome.

In light of this concern, I thought it might be helpful (to those who are close to me, and to others who have considered the vexed questions dividing Orthodox Christians and Roman Catholics) for me to explain what I discovered that made me leave Roman Catholicism, why I rejoined the Orthodox Church, and what difference it makes.

I write this not out of malice toward Roman Catholics. My fondest hope, in fact, is that this will be the beginning of a mutually fruitful discussion to the spiritual benefit of all. As the largest Christian body in the world, with a long and often quite unhappy history of interaction with the Orthodox Church, Roman

Catholicism's differences with Orthodoxy should not lead us to lose sight of the fact that we are all striving to love and serve Jesus Christ and bring His light to the world. But out of respect for God, Who is Truth itself, those differences must not be ignored or papered over either.

Among the differences between Orthodoxy and the primary Roman Catholic doctrines that led to schism from Orthodoxy, are those regarding papal authority and its stances on the nature of authority in the Church in general. It is those considerations that I will outline here, as a response to the case Roman Catholic apologists make for the papacy; a case that many of them direct toward Orthodox Christians in an attempt to convert them to Roman Catholicism. I hope to show at the same time that the Orthodox understanding of the authority and infallibility of the Church is preferable to the Roman Catholic one on the grounds of both Scripture and Holy Tradition, as well as reason. I'll also explore some of the controverted issues, particularly but not solely the Filioque, that divide the Churches. I'll also explain why the Orthodox position is consonant with Sacred Scripture and the teachings of the Holy Fathers and, quite simply, makes sense.

My intention in doing all this is to illuminate the truth, and offer some pertinent information to both Orthodox and Roman Catholic Christians. I have been told, however, that this is a pointless exercise since most people don't evaluate religious claims rationally. If you're Italian or Irish, you're Roman Catholic. If you're Greek, you're Greek Orthodox, and so on. Religious affiliation is, they say, more akin to racial, tribal, and national identity than to a choice based on a rational consideration of the available evidence.

For many, indeed most people, that is true. And others will consider an inquiry such as this one to be out of step with the times. This is the time for dialogue stressing our similarities, not discussions of what separates us, and even less of who is right in those intramural disagreements. I freely confess to being out of step with the times, and not in sync with what many in both churches consider to be important emphases and approaches to various controverted issues today. I offer this inquiry respectfully based on the proposition that no amount of emphasis on what we have in common will erase our differences. If we wish ultimately to resolve those disagreements, we must bring them out in the open and present our cases.

The Scriptures themselves contain calls to evaluate and defend the faith on rational terms. St. Peter tells believers "be ready always to give an answer to every man that asketh you a reason of the hope that is in you..." (I Peter 3:15) And when Paul came to Thessalonica, "where was a synagogue of the Jews: And Paul, as his manner was, went in unto them, and three sabbath days reasoned with them out of the scriptures, opening and alleging, that Christ must needs have suffered, and risen again from the dead; and that this Jesus, whom I preach unto you, is Christ." (Acts 17:1-3) He was not generally well received there, so he went on to Berea, "who coming thither went into the synagogue of the Jews. These were more noble than those in Thessalonica, in that they received the word with all readiness of mind, and searched the scriptures daily, whether those things were so." (Acts 17:10-11)

Some will disparage this entire endeavor, saying that such matters as are considered in this book are best left to theologians, and I am not one. That is true. I don't claim to replace or supersede or outdo the various Roman Catholic-Orthodox theological commissions that are holding discussions today. This book is intended simply to raise questions based on certain available evidence in the hope of leading some people to the truth.

Others will say that since I have been on both sides of this issue, I cannot be trusted as an analyst. To that, I would respond that it is precisely 'because' I have been on both sides of this issue, and can see clearly each side's arguments, that this book has any of the merit it may possess. In any case, the evidence I present here stands on its own, regardless of who has produced it. I hope that it will be evaluated on its own merits.

In writing this book, I have tried at all times to 'speak the truth in love' and help all members of the Holy Orthodox Church, including myself, to "grow up into him in all things, which is the head, even Christ." (Ephesians 4:15)

The Chiefs of the Apostles jointly establishing the Church

CHAPTER ONE

The Role of Saint Peter in the New Testament

THE PROBLEM OF AUTHORITY

Orthodox, Roman Catholics, and Protestants disagree with one another on, among other things, the question of who has authority in the church, and of what that authority consists.

Protestants, the youngest of the three groups, generally hold to the idea known as *sola scriptura*: Scripture alone is and ought to be the only authority in the Church.

Roman Catholics and Orthodox have never held to the *sola scriptura* doctrine for several reasons. Among them is the fact that the New Testament Church, as depicted in the Acts of the Apostles, existed without the portions of New Testament Scripture that had not as yet been written; the Church predates the Scriptures, and the Scriptures are a product of the Church, not the other way around. Protestants would never have known even which books made up their Scripture were it not for the apostolic Church.

What's more, Scripture doesn't interpret itself. Both Orthodox and Roman Catholics, unlike Protestants, recognize that the bishops of the Church, as successors of the apostles, have a certain teaching authority within the Church, to settle disputed questions and determine what is the faith and what is not. Both believe that in this, the Holy Spirit guides the Church, as per the words of Christ, "I have yet many things to say unto you, but ye cannot bear them now. Howbeit when he, the Spirit of truth, is come, he will guide you into all truth..." (John 16:12-13)

Both Orthodox and Roman Catholics also believe that the Church, because of this guidance of the Holy Spirit, is infallible when it makes definitive decisions on the contents of the faith. They agree that ecumenical councils, gatherings of all the world's bishops (or, in practice, as many as practicable), possess this infallibility. Then Catholicism goes farther, insisting that the Pope, as Bishop of Rome and successor of St. Peter, is the first bishop, the earthly head of the Church, and on his own possesses that infallibility when defining dogmas concerning faith and morals.

That is one of the key differences between Orthodox and Roman Catholics, and so is the first topic we will consider. Did the Lord Jesus give St. Peter special authority in the Church? Does this authority pass on to the bishops of Rome? And, lastly, is the Pope infallible when he defines doctrine?

THE ROLE OF PETER

The primary New Testament passages that Roman Catholics use to support the claim that Peter had a unique role among the apostles are Matthew 16:18-20, Luke 22:32, and John 21:15-17.

In the passage from Matthew, the Lord Jesus says to Peter, "And I say also unto thee, That thou art Peter [Greek *Petros*, a masculine form of the word petra, rock], and upon this rock [*petra*] I will build my church; and the gates of hell shall not prevail against it. And I will give unto thee the keys of the kingdom of heaven: and whatsoever thou shalt bind on earth shall be bound in heaven: and whatsoever thou shalt loose on earth shall be loosed in heaven."

Later in the same Gospel, the Lord says much the same thing to the apostles, "Verily I say unto you, Whatsoever ye shall bind on earth shall be bound in heaven." (Matthew18:18) So the controversy centers on the significance of Jesus' giving Peter the name "Rock," and likewise giving him the "keys." Was the Lord conferring a particular authority on Peter that was to be passed on to his successors and form the foundation for the papal monarchy? Or were these singular honors conferred upon Peter alone? Or is there some other explanation altogether?

The Roman Catholic interpretation of the passage is that Jesus meant to give Peter a particular authority among the apostles and primacy over the whole

Church, which special authority and primacy he passed on through apostolic succession to the bishops of Rome. This primacy is confirmed after the resurrection when Jesus tells Peter solemnly three times to "Feed my sheep." (John 21:15-17) This special authority included infallibility, as Jesus has prayed in particular for Peter, that his "faith fail not." (Luke 22:32)

Orthodox theologians tend to see the "rock" not as the person of Peter, but his confession of faith, or Christ Himself. This is not an innovation. The idea of the rock being Christ is taught by St. Peter himself, who is clearly speaking of the Lord Jesus when he writes of "a stone of stumbling, and a rock of offence" (I Peter 2:8). St. Jerome also teaches this. Blessed Augustine, meanwhile, teaches that the rock is the Church and Peter is the prototype for the episcopate. These interpretations are not contradictory but mutually complementary. It is noteworthy, however, that while there are many statements of the Holy Fathers about the preeminence of Peter, nowhere to be found is that Peter is the rock in his very flesh and bones, such that it is his presence in Rome and martyrdom that elevates the See of Rome above all others.

Likewise, Orthodox theologians understand the "feed my sheep" passage as being a threefold reversal of Peter's threefold denial of his Lord on the night of the crucifixion; it was a manifestation of the Lord's mercy, not a conferral of authority. This is confirmed by the fact that Peter was "grieved" by the Lord's thrice-repeated question, "Do you love me?", He was not, in other words, honored or overawed at being given such a great responsibility. Clearly, Peter himself did not think at the moment that this happened that he was being made the pope.

Likewise, the Lord's prayer that Peter's faith "may not fail" was in anticipation of his denial that he knew Jesus when the Roman guards came to arrest him. It was not a conferral of authority, but an acknowledgment that Peter would be the only apostle besides Judas to deny his Master. What's more, the most famous commentary on the meaning of John 21 is in St. John Chrysostom's *On the Priesthood*, in which St. John states that by asking Peter "Do you love Me?" and then saying, "Feed My sheep." The Lord Jesus is establishing the paradigm for priests: that He will measure their love for Him by how they love His flock.

THE RECORD OF THE REST OF THE NEW TESTAMENT

These are, of course, short summaries of arguments that have been made on both sides for hundreds of years. Many have claimed to have the definitive explanation of these passages, but no exegesis has ever been convincing enough to both sides to heal the schism—no doubt because, as we have noted, for many people, religious affiliation is indeed not a matter of rational investigation, but of ethnic or tribal loyalty, or family, or culture. It's something you're born with, and that's that.

But those who do wish to consider these differing interpretations on a rational basis would do well to consider how they were understood by those in a better position than anyone else in the world to know what they really meant: the apostles and those who succeeded them in the leadership of the first-century Church.

And so turning to the Acts of the Apostles, we find a great deal of information about the Church in the months and years immediately following the resurrection of Christ, including a great deal about the activity of St. Peter. Do we find the apostles and the Christian faithful, with Jesus' words about Peter being the "rock" and holding the "keys to the kingdom of heaven" ringing in their ears, treating Peter with the deference due to the "Holy Father," and according him the reverence and respect that is given to the popes today?

Certainly, Peter is in Acts treated with great respect, and his authority as an apostle is recognized, and he is first among the apostles, but even he doesn't seem to be aware that he is the infallible pope, the earthly head of the universal Church. The clearest indication of this comes in the apostolic council, the proceedings of which are detailed in Acts 15. The question before the apostles is whether Gentile converts to Christianity should be required to observe the Mosaic law of the Old Testament. Peter speaks first, followed by Barnabas and Paul. Then James, the brother of the Lord, gives his own assessment, concluding, "Wherefore my sentence ['judgement' ESV] is, that we trouble not them, which from among the Gentiles are turned to God: But that we write unto them, that they abstain from pollutions of idols, and from fornication, and from things strangled, and from blood." (Acts 15:19-20)

My old friend Patrick Madrid, in his defense of papal claims, entitled *Pope Fiction*, says of this council that, "St. Peter's dogmatic pronouncement was accepted and caused all disputes to cease at the Council of Jerusalem (Acts 15)[1]." But if that were the case, then why did Barnabas, Paul, and above all, James, speak after Peter? If Peter's assessment had been understood and accepted as a dogmatic pronouncement, why didn't the assembled apostles and presbyters write to the churches immediately after Peter spoke, informing them of the judgment of the Rock on which the Church was built?

What's more, St. James refers to his own view as "my judgment," which he is giving to the council. He doesn't say something like, "In my opinion, Your Holiness, your judgment should be..." or "Holy Father, I hope that you will decide the question in this way..." The point is not that those titles weren't used; they didn't come into use for many centuries. The point is that no one present seems to have had any idea that the one in the room who had authority over all of them and the ultimate power to make a judgment [or sentence] was Peter. James offers his view as the one that settles the question, and no one contradicts him. He was, in fact, Bishop of Jerusalem and  so had every right to give the judgment at a council held within the area of his responsibility. In fact, his wishes are immediately carried out: the assembly immediately drafts a letter to the churches, as he had directed.

The letter is addressed from "the brethren, both the apostles and the elders, to the brethren who are of the Gentiles in Antioch and Syria and Cilicia" (Acts 15:23). No mention is made of the chief of the apostles, the ultimate authority in the Church, being in their midst and having rendered an infallible judgment. The judgment didn't even come from him, and the letter is addressed from the apostles and elders as if they were a collegial body.

---

1. Pope Fiction, p. 32.

The importance of this cannot be exaggerated, for the apostles who were present at this council recorded in Acts were also present when the Lord said to Peter, "Thou art Peter, and upon this rock I will build my church." If anyone knew what Jesus meant, it was they above all others. Yet instead of behaving as if Peter were the first Pope, the infallible arbiter of the faith and the chief of all the apostles, St. Paul (who was, of course, not present when Jesus said these things, but knew well what had been said, and was in a position to have heard it from the eyewitnesses themselves) even dared to rebuke Peter when he was wrong.

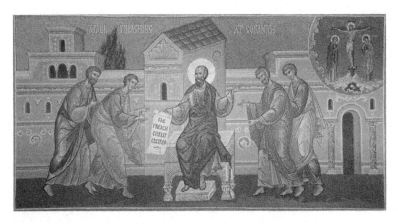

Says Paul: "But when Peter was come to Antioch, I withstood him to the face, because he was to be blamed. For before that certain came from James, he did eat with the Gentiles: but when they were come, he withdrew and separated himself, fearing them which were of the circumcision." (Galatians 2:11-12)

Patrick Madrid rightly argues that this passage does nothing to disprove the Roman Catholic view of papal infallibility, for the First Vatican Council's definition of that doctrine says that the pope is protected from error when speaking *ex cathedra*, that is, in his capacity as the head of the church on earth, on a matter of faith and morals—that is, it covers teaching only, not actions. Popes are supposedly infallible, free from error (in certain carefully defined circumstances); they're not impeccable (free from sin). Paul is rebuking Peter not for teaching error, but for not living up to his own teaching as articulated at the apostolic council. He's not calling him a heretic; he's calling him a hypocrite.

That is true, but it is actually beside the point. The most striking aspect of this incident is that Paul dared to issue the rebuke at all. If Peter had been the pope, with all that Roman Catholics understand the pope to be, is it likely that Paul would have spoken to him in this way? Madrid has to go to the year 1376, when Catherine of Siena scolded Pope Gregory XI, to find even one example of anyone daring to rebuke a pope, and that's the only example he offers.

Even today, when many Roman Catholics are gravely worried that Pope Francis has taught heresy, cardinals have approached the pope with immense hesitation, avoiding any hint of a rebuke, hastening to reaffirm their loyalty and certainty that he has not fallen into heresy, and couching their concerns as questions that they hope he will clarify.

The atmosphere couldn't be more different from Paul's rebuke of Peter. The pope, in his various communications, addresses the Roman Catholic bishops as "venerable brethren," but they are not in any functional sense his brethren. They address him as "Holy Father," and they are indeed much more like children than like brothers before him. A brother may feel free to speak up and correct a brother when he is in error; for a child to correct his father would be presumptuous and insolent.

Of course, a great deal of time has passed since the days of the New Testament. There has been a considerable evolution in Roman Catholicism in its understanding of the role and prerogatives of the papacy, and so Roman Catholics may object that I am being anachronistic when I point out that one doesn't see anything like the papacy in the way the other apostles interacted with St. Peter. But the authority of St. James at the apostolic council and Paul's rebuke of Peter don't indicate simply a less developed understanding of the papal primacy. There is no papal primacy there at all: no indication whatsoever that Peter occupies a place above the other apostles, and considerable evidence to the contrary.

THE HOLY FATHERS' UNDERSTANDING OF THE ROLE OF ST. PETER

A majority of early Church writers view St. Peter as having some preeminence among the Holy Apostles. Tertullian writes in passing that the Church is "built on" St. Peter.[2] Clement of Alexandria calls St. Peter "the chosen, the preeminent,

---

2. Tertullian, Monogamy, 8.4.

the first among the disciples."[3] Origen refers to Peter as the one "upon whom is built the Church of Christ."[4] (All three of those writers have been condemned for various heterodox teachings; I am not quoting them here because they were Orthodox, but because they reflect what was a common understanding in their time about the role of St. Peter.) St. Cyprian of Carthage notes that while the Lord "assigns a like power to all the Apostles, yet He founded a single chair,

and He established by His own authority a source and an intrinsic reason for that unity. Indeed, the others were that also which Peter was; but a primacy is given to Peter, whereby it is made clear that there is but one Church and one chair."[5]

We could multiply examples of this, but they all make the same point. None of the Fathers denied that St. Peter was given primacy in the Church. However, Roman Catholic apologists often tend to assume that this means that papal primacy, infallibility, and universal jurisdiction were given by our Lord

---

3. St. Clement of Alexandria, Who Is the Rich Man That Is Saved?, 21.1.

4. Origen, Commentaries on John, 5.3.

5. St. Cyprian, The Unity of the Catholic Church, 4.

Jesus Christ to St. Peter. Indeed, this is the teaching of the First and Second Vatican Councils.

However, when one examines the teachings of the Fathers, it is by no means a given that Peter's primacy among the apostles equates to the primacy, universal jurisdiction and infallibility of the Bishop of Rome within the Church. Indeed, the evidence is very much to the contrary, as we shall see in the following chapters.

What's more, much of the Roman Catholic case for the pope depends on the idea that the Bishop of Rome is the unique successor of St. Peter and possesses a special role in the Church as a result of that succession. Many Roman Catholic apologetic arguments for the papacy present the case for St. Peter having a unique role, and unique responsibility among the apostles, and then assume on that basis that their case for the unique power of the Bishop of Rome in the Church has been made. We shall see also that while St. Peter does have a key role among the apostles, the early Church by no means took for granted the idea that the Pope of Rome was his successor in a way that others were not.

Saint Ignatius of Antioch

CHAPTER TWO

The Church of Rome in the Pre-Nicene Period

THE EPISTLE OF THE CHURCH OF ROME TO THE CHURCH OF CORINTH

One of the earliest post-New Testament Christian writings is the Epistle to the Corinthians, which dates from the 90s of the first century and is attributed to Clement of Rome, whom you will find on lists of the popes as the fourth pope, the second successor of St. Peter as the Bishop of Rome, after Linus and Cletus. Patrick Madrid notes that, "never is there an outcry from the Church at Corinth complaining that Clement was out of line for presuming to instruct and admonish another preeminent church... The Corinthians complied as best they could with Clement's directives, never once showing shock or resistance to his authority. This is extremely important. If the doctrine of apostolic succession and the primacy of the Roman church was not already understood by Christians of the first century, there would have been an incredible backlash against Clement."[1]

Maybe. If, that is, they knew that he wrote it. The author is actually anonymous; the epistle is addressed from "the Church of God which sojourns at Rome to the Church of God sojourning at Corinth." This is even more important than that Corinth apparently did not protest against receiving this letter. If Clement of Rome, who is traditionally identified as the same Clement whom St. Paul mentions as one of his "fellow labourers" in Philippians 4:3, had written to the Corinthians conscious of his unique authority as the bishop who had the primacy over the whole Church since he was the successor of St.

---

1. Patrick Madrid, Pope Fiction, pp. 74–5.

Peter, why didn't he identify himself in the letter? In the Roman Catholic view, any authority that the Church of Rome had to give direction to the Church of Corinth was due to the prerogatives of the Roman Pontiff, the successor of St. Peter. So if Clement indeed wrote this letter, and was conscious of his authority as the Supreme Pontiff, it would have been only natural for him to identify himself, so that the Corinthians would know that the Pope was speaking to them, and so they should receive his words with the utmost seriousness. But there is no trace of this whatsoever.

One doesn't actually need the papal primacy to explain the Epistle to the Corinthians. Early on in the Church, the churches in great cities began to assume a role of leadership over churches in smaller areas; this eventually developed into the idea of dioceses ruled by a single bishop, and metropolitanates of several bishops under the authority of the bishop of a nearby large city, bishops who came to be known as Patriarchs. The Church of Rome, as the church in the principal city of the Roman Empire, wrote a letter of advice and counsel to the Church of Corinth, a lesser city. In it, the Church of Rome admonishes the Corinthians to, "Submit yourselves to the presbyters."[2] It is silent altogether about any need for the Corinthians to obey the Bishop of Rome as the successor of St. Peter.

THE LETTERS OF ST. IGNATIUS OF ANTIOCH

The preceeding is an argument from silence, and arguments from silence are weak arguments. There may be any number of reasons why the Epistle to the Corinthians doesn't mention the need to obey the Bishop of Rome. Yet this omission might not be so significant if there were not an abundance of other writers of the immediate Post-Apostolic period reminding Christians of their duty to obey the Bishop of Rome. But there aren't. What is striking about this is that the Apostolic Fathers generally do spend a great deal of time telling Christians that they should obey their bishop and his priests; that is, their vision of the Church reflects that of Orthodoxy. St. Ignatius of Antioch in 107, as he was being transported to Rome to be martyred, wrote a series of letters to

---

2. Epistle to the Corinthians, chapter LVII.

churches in various cities; he writes to the Ephesians, "Wherefore it is fitting that you should run together in accordance with the will of your bishop, which thing also you do. For your justly renowned presbytery, worthy of God, is fitted as exactly to the bishop as the strings are to the harp... For if the prayer of one or two possesses such power, how much more that of the bishop and the whole Church!"[3]

To the Trallians he writes in a similar vein, "In like manner, let all reverence the deacons as an appointment of Jesus Christ, and the bishop as Jesus Christ, who is the Son of the Father, and the presbyters as the Sanhedrin of God, and assembly of the apostles. Apart from these, there is no Church."[4] And to the Smyrnaens he is even firmer, "See that ye all follow the bishop, even as Jesus Christ does the Father, and the presbytery as ye would the apostles; and reverence the deacons, as being the institution of God. Let no man do anything connected with the Church without the bishop."[5]

It would be reasonable to expect, in the midst of these admonitions to obey the hierarchy of the Church, to include also the chief hierarch, if one had existed. But St. Ignatius gives no indication in any of his epistles of being aware that there is a bishop of bishops, a bishop with authority over all the others and over the Church as a whole.

Even in his letter to the Church in Rome, Ignatius shows no sign of knowing that he is addressing the seat of the papacy, the Holy See, the summit of all authority in the Church. He does say that the Church of Rome "holds the first place in love," or "presides in love," a phrase which has been made much of by Roman Catholic apologists. However, its very brevity and off-handedness suggests that they are reading too much into it. This phrase is more likely to mean not that the

---

3. St. Ignatius to the Ephesians, chapters 4–5.

4. St. Ignatius to the Trallians, chapter 5.

5. St. Ignatius to the Smyrnaens, chapter 8.

Roman Pontiff, the successor of Peter, resides among the Romans and presides over the whole Church, but that the Roman Church surpasses all the others in charity, or that it holds a priority among the churches for being in the imperial capital. It may be an early indication of the development that resulted in the See of Rome being designated by the Council of Chalcedon in 451 as the first See in the Church, a position it held until the Great Schism of 1054.

St. Ignatius also writes, "I do not, as Peter and Paul, issue commandments unto you. They were apostles; I am but a condemned man: they were free, while I am, even until now, a servant." This is an early confirmation of the Church's belief that both Peter and Paul preached and were martyred in Rome; but here again, St. Ignatius shows no awareness of the Roman Catholic contention that Peter's successors held primacy over the entire Church and the full plenitude of ecclesiastical power.

If something like the Vatican I understanding of the papacy had been present in the Church in St. Ignatius' time, which would only be expected given that Vatican I bases its case upon the New Testament passages above and various texts from the early Church, it strains credulity beyond the breaking point to think that St. Ignatius, who had such a keen concern that Christians would understand the nature and importance of the ordained ministries of bishop, priest, and deacon in the Church, and wrote about these ministries frequently, would refrain from any mention of the papacy even when writing to the very Church in which it was located.

There is not any dispute about these matters. But again, Roman Catholic apologists tend to dismiss this absence by noting that the papacy has been the subject of a development of doctrine. While the truth of the papacy is contained in the deposit of faith delivered to the apostles, they argue, it took centuries for it to be properly understood and elaborated into the modern Holy See. Therefore one should not expect to see the papacy full-blown in the first or second centuries, or even for some time thereafter.

That may be. But it must also be examined as to whether what develops later is indeed a legitimate development, or a corruption, that is, a genuine exposition of a doctrine that was always part of revealed truth, or an interpolation of a doctrine that is not part of the faith and that the Fathers of the Church did not hold.

It is not always easy to distinguish the two; if it were, perhaps the Great Schism would have been healed centuries ago. But the Roman Catholic idea of the development of doctrine is not an assertion that there are new revelations—akin to the claims of the Church of Jesus Christ of Latter-Day Saints. Rather, the development of doctrine refers to the clear elucidation and precise articulation of a doctrine that was always present. Thus we would expect, if the universal jurisdiction and infallibility of the papacy were truly apostolic doctrines held inchoately, that there would be some trace of them, especially given the fact that authority preoccupied the earliest apostolic fathers to a tremendous degree, as they articulated the doctrine of apostolic succession and the threefold order of bishop, priest, and deacon. But these doctrines are not present. In fact, the absence of any mention of Pope or papacy is arresting indeed.

St. Irenaeus of Lyons

In the first three centuries of the Church, however, there is one, and only one, Church Father who appears to speak about, the Roman Church (here again, not specifically the Bishop of Rome) having a superior authority because it is the See of St. Peter. That Church Father is St. Irenaeus of Lyons, who wrote *Against the Heresies* around the year 180. One of the heresies that most preoccupies Irenaeus is that of Gnosticism, which, among other things, claimed to impart a secret teaching of the apostles that had been hidden since their day.

In response, Irenaeus invokes the doctrine of apostolic succession, the idea that the apostles passed on their authority to govern the Church through the laying on of hands (cf. 2 Timothy 1:6) to the bishops, and that those bishops then in the same manner passed on that authority to others. Irenaeus writes, "It is within the power of all, therefore, in every Church, who may wish to see the truth, to contemplate clearly the tradition of the apostles manifested throughout the whole world; and we are in a position to reckon up those who were by the apostles instituted bishops in the churches, and [to demonstrate] the succession of these men to our own times; those who neither taught nor knew of anything like what these [heretics] rave about. For if the apostles had known hidden mysteries, which they were in the habit of imparting to the perfect apart and privily from the rest, they would have delivered them especially to those to whom they were also committing the churches themselves."[6]

Note that Irenaeus speaks of the bishops in the collective. If the papacy with anything like the status and authority it has in Roman Catholic doctrine today had existed at that time, it would have been reasonable for Irenaeus to invoke it in particular, noting that even the successor of St. Peter, infallible in matters of faith and morals, had rejected Gnosticism. Irenaeus does nothing of the sort, although he does speak of the Church of Rome, explaining that he could provide the successions of bishops of all the churches, but that would take too much time, and so he will provide the succession of one prominent church only:

> Since, however, it would be very tedious, in such a volume as this, to reckon up the successions of all the Churches, we do put to confusion all those who, in whatever manner, whether by an evil self-pleasing, by vainglory, or by blindness and perverse opinion, assemble in unauthorized meetings; [we do this, I say,] by indicating that tradition derived from the apostles, of the very great, the very ancient, and universally known Church founded and organized at Rome by the two most glorious apostles, Peter and Paul; as also [by pointing out] the faith preached to men, which comes down to our time by means of the successions of the bishops. For it is a matter of necessity that every Church should agree with this Church, on account of its preeminent authority.[7]

6. St. Irenaeus, Against Heresies, III.3.1.

7. Ibid.

Although this is a foremost proof text for papal authority in the early Church, it is actually a long way from the contemporary Roman Catholic understanding of the primacy and infallibility of the Pope. Irenaeus refers to the Roman Church's having been founded by both Peter and Paul, when according to Roman Catholic doctrine, the Pope's authority derives solely from his being the successor of Peter. In fact, in 1647, Pope Innocent X declared "heretical" the proposition that there was "an exact equality between St. Peter and St. Paul, without subordination and subjection of St. Paul to St. Peter in supreme power, and in the rule of the universal Church."[8] Yet Irenaeus presents them only as "two glorious apostles," without appearing aware of any necessity to present Peter alone as the founding apostle and most important figure of the Church in Rome.

Irenaeus, however, does say that, "every Church should agree with" the Church of Rome, and spokesmen for the papacy have made much of that for centuries.

But is that really what he said? It could be, but it also might not be. The Latin text is, "*Ad hanc enim ecclesiam propter potiorem principalitatem necesse est omnem convenire ecclesiam.*" The word that is translated "agree with" is *convenire*, which could mean "come with" or "belong" as well as "agree with." In other words, Irenaeus could simply be saying that since Rome was the capital of the empire, all the Churches had to have contact with the Church of Rome.

If, on the other hand, he meant that the Bishop of Rome possessed infallibility when defining dogmas regarding faith and morals, it is striking yet again that in many other writings about authority in the Church, Irenaeus never mentions the papacy or the Church of Rome at all.

And other prominent Churchmen of the time display no awareness of the idea that they must in all things "agree with" the Church of Rome.

St. Polycarp in Rome

Shortly after this much-disputed passage, Irenaeus recounts that St. Polycarp, the Bishop of Smyrna, who was martyred in the year 156, traveled to

---

8. Denzinger 1091.

Rome, where he met with Anicetus, the Bishop of Rome, and "caused many to turn away from the aforesaid heretics to the Church of God, proclaiming that he had received this one and sole truth from the apostles—that, namely, which is handed down by the Church."[9] Significantly, Irenaeus doesn't mention any action of Anicetus' own to curb the heretics, a curious omission if it was his primary responsibility to do so as the successor of Peter.

What else happened while Polycarp was in Rome is even more remarkable. The fourth-century ecclesiastical historian Eusebius quotes at length from a letter of Irenaeus about the fact that Polycarp and Anicetus could not come to an agreement over the date of Easter. The churches of Asia Minor celebrated it on the fourteenth day of the month of Nisan, the date of the actual Resurrection, while the Church of Rome insisted that it had to be celebrated on a Sunday.

According to Eusebius, Irenaeus wrote:

> When the blessed Polycarp was at Rome in the time of Anicetus, and they disagreed a little about certain other things, they immediately made peace with one another, not caring to quarrel over this matter. For neither could Anicetus persuade Polycarp not to observe what he had always observed with John the disciple of our Lord, and the other apostles with whom he had associated; neither could Polycarp persuade Anicetus to observe it as he said that he ought to follow the customs of the presbyters that had preceded him.[10]

Anicetus couldn't persuade Polycarp, and it doesn't seem to have occurred to him to order Polycarp to obey him, since, as Vatican II says, "religious submission of mind and will must be shown in a special way to the authentic

---

9. St. Irenaeus, III.3.4.
10. Eusebius, Ecclesiastical History 5.24.16.

magisterium of the Roman Pontiff."[11] Clearly, Anicetus and Polycarp were meeting as equals, not as a superior meeting a subordinate. And Polycarp has no idea that he has any obligation to agree with the Church of Rome; nor does Irenaeus mention any such obligation in his account of the events.

POPE VICTOR

The controversy over the date of Easter continued, but around 190, a new Bishop of Rome resolved to settle it. According to Eusebius, Bishop Polycrates of Ephesus wrote to Pope Victor of Rome, invoking the names of great apostles and saints who had lived and died in Asia Minor, concluding:

> All these observed the fourteenth day of the passover according to the Gospel, deviating in no respect, but following the rule of faith. And I also, Polycrates, the least of you all, do according to the tradition of my relatives, some of whom I have closely followed. For seven of my relatives were bishops; and I am the eighth. And my relatives always observed the day when the people put away the leaven.[12]

What he says next suggests that he had received a previous communication about this, apparently from Pope Victor, and yet was not going to back down even in the face of papal authority:

> I, therefore, brethren, who have lived sixty-five years in the Lord, and have met with the brethren throughout the world, and have gone through every Holy Scripture, am not affrighted by terrifying words. For those greater than I have said, 'We ought to obey God rather than man'... I could mention the bishops who were present, whom I summoned at your desire; whose names, should I write them, would constitute a great multitude. And they, beholding my littleness, gave their consent

---

11. Second Vatican Council, Lumen Gentium 25.
12. Eusebius, 5.24.6.

to the letter, knowing that I did not bear my gray hairs in vain, but had always governed my life by the Lord Jesus.[13]

Victor's reaction to this was to escalate the controversy. Eusebius writes:

Thereupon Victor, who presided over the church at Rome, immediately attempted to cut off from the common unity the parishes of all Asia, with the churches that agreed with them, as heterodox; and he wrote letters and declared all the brethren there wholly excommunicate.[14]

About this, Patrick Madrid writes, "The fact that no bishop in the world— *not a single one*—disputed his authority as bishop of Rome to carry out such an excommunication is a powerful piece of evidence that the early Church recognized the unique authority of the bishop of Rome."[15]

That isn't, however, necessarily so. Eusebius goes on to note that Victor's decision, "did not please all the bishops. And they besought him to consider the things of peace, and of neighborly unity and love. Words of theirs are extant, sharply rebuking Victor."[16]

It's true that Eusebius doesn't record the bishops saying that Victor had no right to excommunicate the Asian churches. Nonetheless, their rejection of that right may be contained in the fact that the excommunications "did not please" them, and that they "sharply rebuked Victor."

To see this more clearly, simply imagine if a group of Roman Catholic bishops had opposed Pope Pius IX's definition of the Immaculate Conception as a divinely revealed dogma of the faith in 1854. Can you imagine these bishops writing to Pius and explaining that they were "not pleased" with his definition, and "sharply rebuking" him? The scenario is inconceivable. When papal infallibility was voted on among the bishops of the First Vatican Council in 1870, 88 bishops voted against it, although many assured the Pope that they simply thought it was inopportune to define it at that time. Ultimately, 60 left

13. Eusebius, 5.24.7–8.
14. Eusebius, 5.24.9.
15. Madrid, 120.
16. Eusebius, 5.24.10.

Rome rather than be compelled to approve the final document. None, however, dared to declare that they were not pleased with the doctrine, or to rebuke Pope Pius IX.

This was not just because Pope Pius IX was a maximalist regarding papal authority. It just was not part of Roman Catholic culture to consider that anyone, even a bishop, could "sharply rebuke" a pope. And this culture didn't arise in a vacuum; it was a product of the Catholic elaboration of the nature of papal authority.

What's more, one of the dissenters from Pope Victor's Easter decision was none other than Irenaeus himself, the bishop who wrote that all churches "must agree" with the Church of Rome. Eusebius recounts:

> Among them was Irenaeus, who, sending letters in the name of the brethren in Gaul over whom he presided, maintained that the mystery of the resurrection of the Lord should be observed only on the Lord's day. He fittingly admonishes Victor that he should not cut off whole churches of God which observed the tradition of an ancient custom...[17]

Eusebius then quotes Irenaeus' letter to Victor, explaining why the pope should not excommunicate the churches of Asia Minor over the date of Easter. His account of St. Polycarp and Pope Anicetus agreeing to disagree on this matter comes from this letter. Irenaeus concludes, "But though matters were in this shape, they communed together, and Anicetus conceded the administration of the eucharist in the church to Polycarp, manifestly as a mark of respect. And they parted from each other in peace, both those who observed, and those who did not, maintaining the peace of the whole church."[18]

This sounds like an amicable meeting of two equals, not a subordinate reporting to his superior.

Most importantly of all, the controversy over the date of Easter was not settled by Pope Victor's decree. It continued long after his death, until finally it was settled at the First Ecumenical Council of Nicaea in 325. What that

17. Eusebius, 5.24.11.
18. Eusebius, 5.24.17.

council stated exactly is not known; however, the Synod of Antioch in 341 decreed, "Whoever shall presume to set aside the decree of the holy and great Synod which was assembled at Nicaea in the presence of the pious Emperor Constantine, beloved of God, concerning the holy and salutary feast of Easter; if they shall obstinately persist in opposing what was [then] rightly ordained, let them be excommunicated and cast out of the Church."[19]

It was an ecumenical council, not a papal decree, that finally laid this matter to rest.

St. Cyprian

In the middle of the third century, another controversy arose. St. Cyprian, Bishop of Carthage, and St. Stephen, Pope of Rome, disagreed over whether those who had been baptized by heretical groups needed to be re-baptized. The controversy between them is also important for it reveals a great deal about how the Fathers of the Church viewed the Bishop of Rome.

In the year 250, Cyprian wrote:

> Our Lord, whose precepts we ought to fear and observe, determines the honour of a bishop and the order of His Church, when He speaks in the Gospel, and says to Peter: "I say to you, that you are Peter, and upon this rock I will build my Church, and the gates of hell will not overcome it. And I will give you the keys of the kingdom of heaven; and whatever things you bind on earth shall be bound also in heaven, and whatever you loose on earth, they shall be loosed also in heaven." [Matthew 16:18-19, ESV] Thence, through the changes of times and successions, the ordination of bishops and the plan of the Church flow on, so that the Church is settled on the bishops, and every act of the Church is regulated by these same prelates. Since then this is founded on divine law, I marvel that some, with bold daring, have ventured to write to meas if

---

19. Synod of Antioch, Canon 1.

they wrote in the name of the Church; whereas the Church is
established in the bishop, and clergy, and all who stand fast. [20]

This might seem at first glance to be an unqualified statement of the primacy
of the Bishop of Rome, but it isn't. After speaking of this passage in Matthew
that is so important for Roman Catholic claims, Cyprian makes no mention
at all of the Pope of Rome. Instead, he speaks of the bishops in the aggregate.
Cyprian clearly understood all bishops, not just the one in Rome, to be
successors of St. Peter. This is clear from other statements Cyprian made: in
252, writing to his fellow bishop, Antonian of Numidia, about the controversy
over whether those who had denied their faith in Christ under pressure from
Roman authorities needed to be baptized, Cyprian speaks of "one episcopate,
diffused through a harmonious multitude of many bishops." [21]

Cyprian added that the question had to be settled, "in a full conference
of bishops, presbyters, deacons, and
confessors, with the laity who have stood
fast." [22] This suggests the Orthodox theology
that an ecumenical council is needed in
order to settle great matters of faith; Cyprian
does not think to appeal to the Pope of
Rome to settle the matter, even though he
is writing to Antonian about, among other
things, his communications with the Roman
Church about this question. Cyprian adds
that the bishops of Africa have already
assembled to discuss this matter, and "lest
the number of bishops in Africa should

seem insufficient, we wrote to Rome on this subject to our colleague Cornelius,
who himself likewise, in a council held with very many fellow bishops, agreed in
the same opinion with us." [23]

---

20. St. Cyprian, Ep. 33.
21. St. Cyprian, Ep. 55.
22. Ibid.
23. St. Cyprian, Ep. 55.

Cyprian not only assumes a conciliar theology; he also assumes that Pope Cornelius holds the same views. Cornelius, as the Pope, had no need to assemble a council of bishops of his own—if, that is, he had any idea that he possessed the powers and authority that Roman Catholicism ascribes to the popes today, but clearly he did not.

As we have seen, other statements of Cyprian support the view that he thought of all bishops collectively as the successors of St. Peter. Christ, he said, "founded one chair, and by his authority appointed the source and system of unity. Certainly, the rest were as Peter was, but primacy is given to Peter, and one Church and one chair is shown: and they are all shepherds, but one flock is exhibited, which is fed by all the apostles with unanimous consent."[24] The one flock is fed by all the apostles; Cyprian makes no mention of any chief bishop or super-apostle who is uniquely the successor of Peter.

During his controversy with Pope Stephen, Cyprian complained that Stephen was "deceived" on the question of the baptism of the lapsed.[25] Even admitting the possibility that the Pope of Rome could be deceived on a matter of faith indicated that Cyprian did not believe he possessed infallibility on such matters. Cyprian added, "Even Peter, whom the Lord first chose and upon whom He built His Church, when Paul later disputed with him over circumcision, did not claim insolently any prerogative for himself, nor make any arrogant assumptions, nor say that he had the primacy and ought to be obeyed the more by novices and newcomers."[26]

Peter did not say he had the primacy; clearly, Cyprian believed that Pope Stephen should not either. The bishops of Africa agreed. On September 1, 256, 87 bishops of Africa, led by Cyprian, met in the Council of Carthage and issued a judgment on the vexed question of the baptism of heretics. In a direct rebuke of Pope Stephen, the bishops declared:

> It remains for each one of us to say what he thinks on this
> subject, judging no one, nor depriving anyone of the right of
> communion, if he should think differently. For no one among

---

24. St. Cyprian, The Unity of the Catholic Church, 4.
25. St. Cyprian, Epistle 67.
26. St. Cyprian, Epistle 71.

us sets himself up as a bishop of bishops, or by tyranny and terror forces his colleagues to compulsory obedience, seeing that every bishop in the freedom of his liberty and power possesses the right to his own mind and can no more be judged by another than he himself can judge another. We must all await the judgment of our Lord Jesus Christ, who singly and alone has power both to appoint us to the government of his Church and to judge our acts therein.[27]

A stronger denial of the papal prerogatives as Vatican **I** and Vatican **II** envision them could scarcely be imagined.

---

27. Council of Carthage.

The First Ecumenical Council, Nicaea

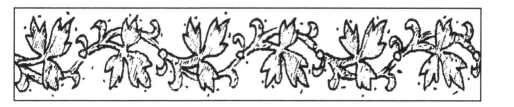

CHAPTER THREE

The Holy Fathers and the Councils of Nicaea and Constantinople

THE COUNCIL OF NICAEA

The First Ecumenical Council, held in Nicaea in the year 325, offers no more comfort for the defenders of the modern papacy. Its famous Canon 6 is the only one that mentions the authority of the Bishop of Rome:

> Let the ancient customs in Egypt, Libya and Pentapolis prevail, that the Bishop of Alexandria have jurisdiction in all these, since the like is customary for the Bishop of Rome also. Likewise in Antioch and the other provinces, let the Churches retain their privileges. And this is to be universally understood, that if anyone be made bishop without the consent of the Metropolitan, the great Synod has declared that such a man ought not to be a bishop. If, however, two or three bishops shall from natural love of contradiction, oppose the common suffrage of the rest, it being reasonable and in accordance with the ecclesiastical law, then let the choice of the majority prevail.

There are several important aspects to this. The first, once again, is the absence of any reference to any universal primacy or infallibility of the Pope of Rome. Second, the opening part of the canon grants metropolitan jurisdiction, that is, authority over the neighboring dioceses, to the Bishop of Alexandria, and mentions that the Bishop of Rome likewise has such jurisdiction. Not jurisdiction over the whole Church, but presumably only jurisdiction over the lesser sees in Italy neighboring Rome. The Council does not seem to be aware that the Pope of Rome has any greater authority than that which they are affirming for the Bishop of Alexandria.

Moreover, bishops are warned against daring to "oppose the common suffrage of the rest." That is, they are being directed to accept the judgment of the whole, which settles matters that are under dispute. No mention is made of any obligation that those who possess a "natural love of contradiction" have to obey the Roman Pontiff.

Note also that the Council was held in Nicaea, near Constantinople, not in Rome. Of the fourteen councils that Roman Catholics hold to be ecumenical that the Orthodox Church rejects, seven have been held in Rome, and two others nearby in Italy. This is to be expected, given the role the pope has in Roman Catholicism. But none of the seven ecumenical councils which are accepted by both Orthodox Christians and Roman Catholics were held in Rome; no one seems to have the idea that since Rome was the See of the Vicar of Christ, the Supreme Pontiff, that it would be the best logical place for an ecumenical council. Nor did the pope preside over those councils, as he did at Vatican I and Vatican II; no popes even attended the seven ecumenical councils, and the legates they sent did not preside over these councils—another curious fact if it had been recognized that "the Roman church possesses a pre-eminence of ordinary power over every other church," as Vatican I states.[1]

POPE JULIUS I

After the Council of Nicaea, Arian heretics drove St. Athanasius, the Bishop of Alexandria, from his See. In 339, Athanasius sailed to Rome, which was still the primary city in the empire; the Emperor Constantine had moved his imperial capital to Constantinople only nine years before. Pope Julius of Rome wrote to the party of Arianizing bishops who opposed Athanasius, who were known as the Eusebians, telling them that the views he had previously expressed on the controversy were, "not only mine, but that of all the bishops throughout Italy and in these parts."[2]

---

1. First Vatican Council, Pastor Aeternus 2.
2. Pope Julius, To the Eusebians, 26.

Why would this assurance be necessary if the pope's judgments were known to be sufficient in themselves? No pope in modern times, or for many, many centuries, has ever felt it necessary to invoke the fact that other bishops agree with him to support the correctness of his views. In fact, in defining papal infallibility, the First Vatican Council notes that, "such definitions of the Roman Pontiff are irreformable of themselves, and not from the consent of the Church."[3] The Second Vatican Council elaborates on this, "And therefore his definitions, of themselves, and not from the consent of the Church, are justly styled irreformable since they are pronounced with the assistance of the Holy Spirit, promised to him in blessed Peter, and therefore they need no approval of others, nor do they allow an appeal to any other judgment."[4]

Both of these statements refer only to infallible definitions, but it can hardly be maintained that modern-day popes act collegially in the ordinary exercise of their ministry. The ecclesiastical environment in which any pope would assure his opponents in a theological controversy that his opinion was, "not only mine, but that of all the bishops throughout Italy and in these parts" is a relic of the distant and long-forgotten past.

In the same letter, Pope Julius admonishes the Eusebian bishops: "And why were we not written to, especially about the Church of the Alexandrians? Are you ignorant that the custom was first to write to us, and then for justice to be determined from here?"[5] That judgment, however, was not to be rendered by the successor of Peter exercising his supreme jurisdiction over the whole Church: Julius also writes, "You should have written to us all, so that justice might be determined by all."[6] Not by one.

POPE LIBERIUS

Pope Julius' successor, Liberius, was sent into exile in 355 for his defense of Athanasius. Under severe pressure, and, according to St. Jerome, "giving in to the irksomeness of exile," reversed the judgment of his predecessor, condemned

---

3. Pastor Aeternus 4.
4. Lumen Gentium 25.
5. Pope Julius, 35.
6. Ibid., 35.

Athanasius, and endorsed Arianism. He wrote to the Arian bishops and priests in the East denying that he had ever supported Athanasius:

> I did not defend Athanasius, but because my predecessor Julius, of good memory, had received him, I was afraid lest I might be judged a dissembler of some sort. But when, by God's will, I realized that you had justly condemned him, I at once assented to your opinions... So then, Athanasius being removed from communion with all of us, and since I am not even to receive his letters, I say that I am quite at peace with all of you...[7]

It is generally acknowledged that Pope Liberius condemned Athanasius and accepted Arianism only under severe duress from the Emperor Constantius II. The Orthodox Church reveres Pople Liberius as a saint and regards him not as a heretic, but as a defender of Orthodoxy. So his disavowal of Athanasius and entry into communion with Arian bishops is no argument against papal prerogatives as Roman Catholics define them today.

However, his letter once again reveals a completely different ecclesiastical world from that in which the Holy Father in Rome makes judgments and the Church accepts them. Liberius writes to the Eusebians describing how he "assented" to their opinions; he appears to take for granted that he is one of a group of bishops, and that general agreement among bishops is a positive good, even if it is obtained by his coming around to agreement with a group, rather than that bishops, and all the faithful, need to come around to agreement with him, and that judgment is reserved to him.

What's more, Liberius' lapse from Orthodoxy, whether or not it was under duress, led to no discussion in the Church of his time about what his actions meant, or did not mean, for papal authority and infallibility. Athanasius, in his *History of the Arians*, describes Liberius' initial heroism in standing up to pressure and then how, "from fear of threatened death, he subscribed" to the heresy.[8] Yet, Athanasius adds, "although the ungodly had done all this, yet they

---

7. Pope Liberius, To the Eastern Presbyters and Bishops.
8. St. Athanasius, History of the Arians, 41.

thought they had accomplished nothing, so long as the great Hosius escaped their knavish tricks."[9]

This is an extraordinary statement. The Arians had captured the pope, yet "they thought they had accomplished nothing" unless they also turned Hosius, the venerable Bishop of Cordoba, who was one of the most compelling advocates for the Athanasian theology that the Orthodox had recognized as the true doctrine. Athanasius reveals in this that he has no conception of the pope's authority as anything close to what Roman Catholics today professes it to be; he takes for granted that Liberius was, like Hosius, a key defender of Orthodoxy, and that is why he was of value to the Arians if he could be forced to endorse their position. If Liberius had been the pope the way Pius IX or John Paul II, or Francis were popes, there would have been no need for the Arians to try to force Hosius to align with them as well.

St. Cyril of Jerusalem

Around the year 348, St. Cyril of Jerusalem delivered a series of twenty-three catechetical lectures. In them, he refers to St. Peter as "the chiefest and first of the apostles" and "the leader of the  apostles and chief herald of the Church,"[10] but doesn't say a word about his successors in Rome carrying on his authority as the chief bishop in the Church. In fact, he refers in one lecture to Peter and Paul as "the rulers of the Church," a formulation that contradicts the Roman Catholic view that St. Peter had a unique authority among the apostles.[11]

No defenders of the Roman See ever remonstrated with St. Cyril or denounced him for downplaying the papal prerogatives.

---

9. Athanasius, History of the Arians, 42.

10. St. Cyril of Jerusalem, Lectures 2.19; 11.3.

11. St. Cyril of Jerusalem, Lecture 6.15.

THE FIRST COUNCIL OF CONSTANTINOPLE

No papal legates were even present at the Second Ecumenical Council, the First Council of Constantinople in 381. No attention was paid to this at the time, but imagine Roman Catholics holding an ecumenical council today without notifying the pope or having him or his representatives present. That would be inconceivable, but the First Council of Constantinople was immediately accepted as ecumenical by the Church in both the East and the West, without anyone remarking on how strange it was that neither the pope nor his legates were present.

Canon 3 of this Council states, "Because it is new Rome, the bishop of Constantinople is to enjoy the privileges of honor after the bishop of Rome."[12] Nothing is said about the pope's prerogatives stemming from his being the successor of Peter and inheritor of his plenary power over the Church; the Council assumes that the honor given to the Sees of Rome and Constantinople stems from their importance as capital cities of the Roman Empire.

ST. JOHN CHRYSOSTOM

St. John Chrysostom wrote a great deal about St. Peter's role in the Church, and is often invoked as a strong supporter of papal authority since he wrote that St. Peter was, "the leader of the choir, the mouth of all the apostles, the head of that tribe, the ruler of the whole world, the foundation of the Church."[13] However, in other statements, St. John makes it clear that he does not subscribe to the view that this status of Peter translates to plenary authority and infallibility for the Bishop of Rome, and that his view of St. Peter's role itself is considerably different from that of the First and Second Vatican Councils.

In contrast to the Roman Catholic idea that St. Peter alone, and through him the popes, received the keys of the kingdom of heaven (Matthew 16:19), St. John subscribes to the Orthodox view that the keys were given to all the apostles in the person of St. Peter. St. John Chrysostom describes St. John

---

12. First Council of Constantinople, Canon 3.
13. St. John Chrysostom, Homily on 2 Timothy 3.1.

the Evangelist as "the son of thunder, the beloved of Christ, the pillar of the churches throughout the world, having the keys of heaven."[14]

In a homily on the Apostolic Council of Acts 15, where a replacement for Judas Iscariot was chosen to be the twelfth apostle, St. John notes that St. Peter,  "defers the decision to the whole body."[15] St. John does, however, suggest that Peter had the authority to appoint a new apostle alone, and only refrained from doing so in order to avoid the appearance of favoritism, "Why did it not rest with Peter to make the election himself: what was the motive? This; that he might not seem to bestow it of favor. And besides, he was not yet endowed with the Spirit."[16]

However, St. John states in another homily about the Apostolic Council that St. James, as bishop of Jerusalem, "was invested with the chief rule."[17] He even implies that St. James had a greater authority than St. Peter, "Peter indeed spoke more strongly, but James here more mildly: for thus it behooves one in high authority, to leave what is unpleasant for others to say, while he himself appears in the milder part."[18]

In a homily on St. Paul's Epistle to the Romans, St. John makes it clear that he, like St. Irenaeus, considers the Roman See to be that of both Peter and Paul, not just of Peter alone, in a manner that is difficult to reconcile with the declaration of Pope Innocent X. St. John writes:

> Where the Cherubim sing the glory, where the Seraphim are flying, there shall we see Paul, with Peter, and as a chief

14. St. John Chrysostom, Homily 1 on John.
15. St. John Chrysostom, Homily 3 on the Acts of the Apostles.
16. Ibid.
17. St. John Chrysostom, Homily 33 on the Acts of the Apostles.
18. Ibid.

and leader of the choir of the Saints, and shall enjoy his generous love. For if when here he loved men so, that when he had the choice of departing and being with Christ, he chose to be here, much more will he there display a warmer affection. I love Rome even for this, although indeed one has other grounds for praising it, both for its greatness, and its antiquity, and its beauty, and its populousness, and for its power, and its wealth, and for its successes in war. But I let all this pass, and esteem it blessed on this account, that both in his lifetime he wrote to them, and loved them so, and talked with them whiles he was with us, and brought his life to a close there. Wherefore the city is more notable upon this ground, than upon all others together. And as a body great and strong, it has as two glistening eyes, the bodies of these Saints. Not so bright is the heaven, when the sun sends forth his rays, as is the city of Rome, sending out these two lights into all parts of the world. From thence will Paul be caught up, from thence Peter. Just bethink you, and shudder (φρίξατε) at the thought of what a sight Rome will see, when Paul arises suddenly from that deposit, together with Peter, and is lifted up to meet the Lord.[19]

When St. John Chrysostom was deposed as Patriarch of Constantinople in 405, he wrote for help to Pope Innocent I, and also to the Bishops of Milan and Aquileia. If the Pope of Rome was what the pope is now, why did St. John bother to write to the other bishops? The pope with his plenary power would be able to solve the problem; no one else's help would have been needed. If papal claims were true, St. John Chrysostom's appeal to the Bishops of Milan and Aquileia would be rather like a Roman Catholic bishop under fire today appealing to the bishops of Paris and Vienna as well as to the pope. To do so would be gilding the lily, entirely superfluous.

Moreover, when St. John Chrysostom writes to Pope Innocent, he does not do so as if the pope were the final arbiter and ultimate judge. He was just trying to get some prominent bishops on his side. If the papacy had existed then in the

19. St. John Chrysostom, Homily 32 on Romans.

form it has now, he would have written solely to the pope as the court of final appeal, as everyone involved would have taken for granted that the matter was for the pope to decide, and what the bishops of Milan and Aquileia thought was of no importance.

POPE INNOCENT I

This is not to say that the Bishop of Rome did not have any special place in the Church. As the bishop of the empire's key city, he was increasingly recognized as having primacy among the bishops. The Church historian Sozomen, writing around 450, said that, "the Roman Church was entitled to the honor of all, because it was the school of the apostles and was from the beginning the metropolis of religion, although those who imported the doctrine came to her from the East."[20] Since the Great Schism in which the Church of Rome separated from the Church of Constantinople and the other Eastern Sees, the Ecumenical Patriarch of Constantinople has exercised that primacy of honor. But it does not mean for the Orthodox Church, and did not mean for the Church of the first millennium, that the bishop exercising that primacy had universal jurisdiction over the entire Church, or infallibility in matters of faith and morals.

Regarding infallibility, the First Vatican Council states, "We teach and define that it is a divinely-revealed dogma: that the Roman Pontiff, when he speaks *ex cathedra*, that is, when in discharge of the office of Pastor and Teacher of all Christians, by virtue of his supreme Apostolic authority, he defines a doctrine regarding faith or morals to be held by the Universal Church, by the divine assistance promised to him in blessed Peter, is possessed of that infallibility with which the divine Redeemer willed that His Church should be endowed for defining doctrine regarding faith or morals: and that therefore such definitions of the Roman Pontiff are irreformable of themselves, and not from the consent of the Church."[21]

For a dogmatic definition of the pope to be infallible, he must be speaking *ex cathedra*, that is, "when in discharge of the office of Pastor and Teacher

---

20. Sozomen, Church History, 3.8.
21. Pastor Aeternus, 4.

of all Christians, by virtue of his supreme Apostolic authority, he defines a
doctrine regarding faith or morals to be held by the Universal Church." Since
this definition in 1870, there has been only one papal statement that met these
specifications: Pope Pius XII's definition of the Assumption of the Blessed
Virgin Mary as a dogma of the faith in 1950.

However, throughout the history of the Church, there have been other
papal statements in which the pope was clearly intending to discharge his office
and define a doctrine to be held by the whole Church. Thus, if the First Vatican
Council is to be believed, these, too, must be infallible, protected from error by
the Holy Spirit.

This claim first encounters difficulty with a statement of Pope Innocent I
early in the fifth century. St. Augustine relates that Innocent settled a controversy
regarding the question of whether or not Holy Communion should be given to
infants in no uncertain terms:

> What was that which the same pope replied to the bishops
> of Numidia concerning this very cause, because he had
> received letters from both Councils, as well from the Council
> of Carthage as from the Council of Mileve—does he not speak
> most plainly concerning infants? For these are his words: "For
> what your Fraternity asserts that they preach, that infants can be
> endowed with the rewards of eternal life even without the grace
> of baptism, is excessively silly; for unless they shall eat the flesh
> of the Son of man, and drink His blood, they shall not have
> life in them-selves "Pope Innocent, of blessed memory, says
> that infants have not life without Christ's baptism, and without
> partaking of Christ's body and blood. If he should say, They
> will not, how then, if they do not receive eternal life, are they
> certainly by consequence condemned in eternal death if they
> derive no original sin?[22]

Was Pope Innocent speaking *ex cathedra*? He was responding to letters from
two local councils that were considering this question, and thus clearly exercising

---

22. Blessed Augustine, Two Letters Against the Pelagians, 2.7

his authority, acting—as Vatican I put it, "in discharge of the office of Pastor and Teacher of all Christians, by virtue of his supreme Apostolic authority." Was he intending to define, "a doctrine regarding faith or morals to be held by the Universal Church"? That is clear as well since he says that infants, as Augustine relates Innocent's ruling, "have not life without Christ's baptism, and without partaking of Christ's body and blood." This is clearly a doctrine that Innocent believed to be held, or should be held, by the universal Church: infants can't be cut off from eternal life for not receiving Holy Communion in one jurisdiction and yet free from this risk in another.

The fact that Innocent's statement has apparently not survived outside of Augustine's writings is immaterial. Augustine is not known to be an untrustworthy witness, although he is known to be at odds with other Fathers regarding original sin (or what is known as "ancestral sin" among the Orthodox); and the passage of time is so great that no conclusions can be drawn from the absence of this document in the papal archives, if it is indeed not present there.

What is important about Innocent's statement is that it meets all of Vatican I's criteria for an infallible statement of the Roman Pontiff. Such decisions, says Vatican I, are "irreformable of themselves, and not from the consent of the Church."[23] Yet Roman Catholics did not hesitate to reform it, at the Council of Trent over a thousand years later. That Council taught a flat contradiction of what Pope Innocent had taught, "If anyone says that communion of the Eucharist is necessary for little children before they have attained the years of discretion, let him be anathema."[24]

No doubt by the time of the Council of Trent, Pope Innocent's words had been long forgotten, and the practice of the Roman Church had changed; Holy Communion was no longer given to infants. But if papal infallibility as defined by Vatican I is indeed a divinely revealed dogma, then it had to be a part of the teachings imparted by the apostles to their successors, the first bishops; the Roman Church, like all Christian churches, teaches that revelation ended with the death of the last apostle.

---

23. Pastor Aeternus, 4.
24. Council of Trent, canon 4.

That means there is no time limit. Dogmas are divinely revealed, and as such they do not expire. Truth is eternal and changeless. A is A throughout all ages. If Pope Innocent intended to teach a doctrine that he believed should be held by the whole Church, then it would be a doctrine to be held by the whole Church for all time. The infallibility of the Church is held by the apostolic Churches in both the East and the West; it is a recognition of the Lord's promise that He would send the Holy Spirit, who would not allow the Church to go astray, "Howbeit when he, the Spirit of truth, is come, he will guide you into all truth." (John 16:13).

The only way out of this for defenders of papal infallibility would be to maintain that Pope Innocent was not speaking *ex cathedra*. But which parts of the Vatican I criteria for an *ex cathedra* statement did he not meet? He was responding to letters from local councils who were asking not his personal opinion, but the view of the Pope of Rome on a matter of Christian doctrine. Innocent clearly meant to settle the matter by giving the orthodox view. And when he did so, he characterized the rulings of these local councils as "excessively silly," and warned that unless infants received Holy Communion, they did not have eternal life.

If this was a question of salvation or damnation, it was quintessentially a matter of faith. But if it was indeed such a matter, then the pope's teaching is contradicted by the later Roman Council, which Roman Catholics consider to be an ecumenical council, and so either the pope or the Council is wrong and therefore not infallible. Yet according to Roman Catholic teaching, both popes and Ecumenical Councils are infallible, and so in this contradiction the Roman Catholic teaching on how infallibility is exercised within the Church is thus revealed to be false.

The only other possibility is that Pope Innocent was referring only to baptism, not Holy Communion, as necessary for infant salvation, for it is the idea that infants need not be baptized that he terms "excessively silly," and only introduces the question of Holy Communion after that. However, Augustine's summary statement clearly refers to both sacraments: "Pope Innocent, of blessed memory, says that infants have not life without Christ's baptism, and without partaking of Christ's body and blood." Augustine also speaks elsewhere of the need for infants to receive both baptism and the Holy Eucharist: "If reconciliation through Christ is necessary to all men... This reconciliation is in the laver of regeneration and in the flesh and blood of Christ, without which not even infants can have life in themselves."[25]

Thus it is clear that Augustine understood that the pope meant to say that both sacraments were required for infants, and that Pope Innocent meant to settle a matter of faith for the whole Church. The contradiction of his teaching on this matter by the Council of Trent destroys the entire edifice of papal infallibility.

BLESSED AUGUSTINE

Blessed Augustine of Hippo, the towering early theologian of the Church in the West, is renowned for, among other things, encapsulating the papal

claims of primacy and infallibility in four words: *Roma locuta, causa finita*: Rome has spoken, the matter is finished. Numerous Roman Catholic apologists have pointed to this as evidence that Augustine took it for granted that when the pope ruled on a disputed issue, the dispute was over, and it was up to the faithful simply to accept the pope's judgment.

What Augustine actually wrote was not, "Rome has spoken, the matter is settled," but this, "Two councils on this question have been sent to the Apostolic See; and replies have also come from there. The cause is finished; would that the error might sometime be finished also!"[26] He was speaking of the Pelagian heresy, and saying that the Pelagians had exhausted all their appeals against the judgment that their doctrine was heretical. He was not saying that they were heretical because Rome had said so.

---

25. Blessed Augustine, Two Letters Against the Pelagians, 4.8.
26. St. Augustine, Sermon 131:10.

The proof of this is in Augustine's other writings. Augustine is also the author of a lengthy treatise entitled *On the Unity of the Church*, in which he endeavored to answer this question, "Is the Church of Christ among the Catholics or among the Donatists?" The Donatists were heretics in North Africa who taught that if a bishop or priest was sinful, the prayers and sacraments he offered were invalid. Augustine said that the question of whether the true Church was that of the Catholics or the Donatists, "needs to be determined from specific and clear citations in Holy Scripture." *On the Unity of the Church* is over 30,000 words long, the size of a small book, and yet not once does Augustine say that one must be in communion with the Bishop of Rome as the foundation of the unity of the Church, or obedient to him as the basis of the Church's orthodoxy. He doesn't mention papal authority at all, which is an extraordinarily curious omission if the pope was understood to be, "the perpetual and visible principle and foundation of unity of both the bishops and of the faithful," as Vatican II says.[27]

Discussing the case of a bishop Caecilian, who became the focus of a controversy between the orthodox and the Donatists, Augustine wrote, "Let us suppose that these bishops who decided the case of Caecilian at Rome were not good judges; there still remained a plenary council of the universal Church, in which these judges might themselves be put on their defense, so that, if they were convicted of mistake, their decisions might be reversed."[28] Augustine speaks only of an ecumenical council reviewing the judgment of the bishops; he doesn't mention the possibility that the pope could review the case and issue the final judgment based on his plenary authority. He does not show any awareness that the pope had such authority.

Augustine is also uncertain of the foundational Roman Catholic arguments for papal authority: the claim that in Matthew 16:13-20, the Lord Jesus said He would build the Church on Peter, as its "rock." Augustine acknowledges this interpretation but then says, "What was said to him was not 'You are the rock,' but 'You are Peter.' But the rock was Christ, having confessed whom

---

27. Lumen Gentium 23.
28. St. Augustine, Epistle 43.

(even as the whole Church confesses) Simon was named Peter. Which of these two interpretations is the more likely to be correct, let the reader choose."[29]

POPE ZOSIMUS

In 417, the African Bishop Celestius, an associate of the heretic Pelagius, was condemned by the other bishops of Africa, and appealed to Pope Zosimus. This was in accord with Canon 6 of the Council of Nicaea: the bishops of Africa were within the metropolitan jurisdiction of the See of Rome, so it was entirely justified for Celestius to appeal to the pope. In his letter to Zosimus, Celestius discusses infant baptism and declares, "We did not say that infants, therefore, must be baptized for the remission of sins in order that we might seem to affirm original sin, which is very alien from catholic sentiment. But because sin is not born with a man, it is subsequently committed by the man."[30]

This was a plainly heretical statement, as the Church affirms that all people suffer from original sin, that is, all bear the consequences of the sin of Adam and Eve, the chief of which is death.

Pope Zosimus studied the matter carefully, writing to the African bishops that, "We caused to be recited the pamphlet which he had handed in," denying original sin, and then questioned Celestius extensively, "We repeatedly inquired of him whether he spoke from his heart or with his lips the things he had written." The pope assured the African bishops that, "We have decided nothing hurriedly or immaturely."

Then he praised, "the unfettered faith of Celestius," and challenged Celestius' critics to produce any evidence that, "He now believes otherwise than the contents of his pamphlets and confession."

As in the case of Zosimus' predecessor, Pope Innocent, Roman Catholic apologists claim that Zosimus, in affirming the orthodoxy of a statement denying original sin, was not speaking *ex cathedra*. Here again, however, to make this denial empties the very idea of speaking *ex cathedra* of all its meaning.

29. St. Augustine, Retractions, I.21.
30. Celestius, Libellus, in St. Augustine, On Original Sin, 26.

Was Zosimus giving his personal opinion or speaking as the Pope of Rome? Clearly, he was acting in his official capacity and ruling on a disputed matter. Did he mean to define, "a doctrine regarding faith or morals to be held by the Universal Church?" He was ruling on whether Celestius' teaching was orthodox, and so it was certainly a doctrinal matter. Celestius denied the doctrine of original sin, and so Pope Zosimus, "in discharge of the office of Pastor and Teacher of all Christians, by virtue of his supreme Apostolic authority," was declaring to the African bishops that one could deny the doctrine of original sin and still be an orthodox believer.

To say that this was not declaring a heresy to be the faith of the Church strains credulity. If papal infallibility is not in play when the pope declares whether a statement on a core Christian doctrine is orthodox or heretical, its parameters are so extremely circumscribed as to render it essentially useless. If the pope is only infallible when he formally defines a doctrine, and can be in error even when ruling on doctrinal matters and expecting his ruling to settle a disputed question and be obeyed, then the scope of papal infallibility is so small as to be practically non-existent. But if Pope Zosimus was indeed declaring that a heresy was orthodox, then the Popes of Rome are not infallible in any case.

The African bishops, apparently unaware that they were bound to obey the pope's judgment, were defiant and declared that the judgment of Pope Innocent, who had declared Celestius' doctrines heretical, would stand. Then Zosimus backtracked. In March 418, he wrote to the African bishops a curious letter in which he declared that in view of the authority of the Roman See, "No one can revise our sentence," and then he proceeded to revise it himself. "You have understood the entire text of our letter," he complained, "as if we had believed Celestius in everything, and had given our assent, so to speak, to every syllable without discussing his words." He denied having done so.

However, in his first letter, Pope Zosimus gave no hint that he rejected any part of Celestius' teaching, and was emphatic that he had questioned him carefully about the very document in which the bishop had denied original sin and found his answers satisfactory.

Was papal infallibility saved because Zosimus backtracked from his endorsement of a rejection of original sin? Is there a time limit on erroneous papal rulings, such that if they are retracted within a certain time period, the doctrine of papal infallibility is preserved?

The Pelagians, for their part, were enraged by Zosimus' backtracking and accused him of, "the crime of prevarication."[31] Augustine defended the pope, "What sort of letter or what decree is found of the late Pope Zosimus in which he declared that we must believe that man is born without any taint of original sin? He certainly never said this; he never wrote it at all."[32]

That is true. Pope Zosimus did not issue any such declaration. But he did declare that Celestius, with specific reference to a letter in which Celestius denied the doctrine of original sin, was orthodox. Was that not affirming that the denial of the doctrine of original sin was orthodox? Does the distinction that Augustine is drawing really make an actual distinction in terms of the content of the pope's teaching?

If defenders of papal infallibility will insist, in attempting to exonerate Popes Innocent and Zosimus from doctrinal error, that no papal statement is infallible except those that adhere to the formula found in Pope Pius IX's definition of the Immaculate Conception in 1854 and Pope Pius XII's definition of the Assumption in 1950 ("We declare, state, and define that it is a dogma divinely revealed..."), then those are the only two occasions on which papal infallibility has been exercised. Some Roman Catholics affirm exactly this; others say that other statements, none of which contain this formula, also fit the requirements needed for a statement to be regarded as infallible.

But if other statements, not containing that phrase, can be regarded as exercises of papal infallibility, then the dogmatic errors of Innocent and Zosimus cannot be dismissed simply because the phrase is lacking. And if the two definitions from the nineteenth and twentieth centuries are the only exercises of papal infallibility, then *every other dogma held by the Church has been established by means other than a papal statement.* That in itself should move Roman Catholics to begin to reconsider the entire concept of papal infallibility.

---

31. St. Augustine, Against Two Pelagian Epistles, 5.
32. Ibid.

The Fourth Ecumenical Council, Chalcedon

CHAPTER FOUR

The Holy Fathers and the Councils
of Ephesus and Chalcedon

THE COUNCIL OF EPHESUS

The Third Ecumenical Council was convened in Ephesus in 431 with Cyril, Patriarch of Alexandria, presiding, in order to judge Nestorius, the Patriarch of Constantinople, who had taught that because of the distinction between Christ's human and divine natures, Mary was more properly called "Mother of Christ" (*Christotokos*) than "Mother of God" (*Theotokos*). Pope Celestine had condemned Nestorius in 430 and affirmed the orthodoxy of the term *Theotokos*; if he had been recognized as having the authority that the pope has today, why wasn't that the end of the matter? The Fathers of the Council of Ephesus acknowledged that Pope Celestine already, "gave judgment concerning the present cause and affair..." but that didn't stop them from examining it themselves.[1]

If it had been understood that, "Definitions of the Roman Pontiff are irreformable of themselves, and not from the consent of the Church," as Vatican I says, why did they even bother?[2] But they did, and finding Celestine's judgment coinciding with their own, the assembled bishops exclaimed, "This is a just judgment. To Celestine, the modern Paul! To Celestine, the guardian of the faith! To Celestine, of one mind

---

1. Council of Ephesus, Second Session, July 10, 431.
2. Pastor Aeternus, IV.

with the Synod! To Celestine, the whole Synod offers its thanks! One Celestine! One Cyril! One faith of the Synod! One faith of the world!"[3]

These pious exclamations raise a number of questions. The Fathers say, "This is a just judgment." But here again, Roman Catholic theology holds that papal decisions on matters of faith need no confirmation from anyone. Yet the Fathers of Ephesus clearly assume that it is up to them to determine whether or not Pope Celestine's judgment is orthodox. When they do, they call Celestine, "the modern Paul." They apparently didn't think Celestine's status as successor of St. Peter was his defining and most important  characteristic; their praising of Celestine as a new Paul rather than a new Peter casts an intriguing light on the Council of Chalcedon's exclamations two decades later about Pope Leo the Great—"Peter has spoken through Leo!"—about which much has been made by papal apologists.

Note also that the Council Fathers at Ephesus are rejoicing at the fact that Celestine is "of one mind with the Synod." Shouldn't they have rejoiced rather that the Synod was of one mind with Celestine? They should have rejoiced at their agreement with the pope if ecumenical councils existed in order to ratify the decisions of the Roman Pontiff and cannot issue any statement that has not been approved by him, which is the way that Roman Catholic councils operate. But in the Church before the Great Schism, no one understood that as the way that ecumenical councils worked.

The Council of Ephesus also decreed that "It is unlawful for any man to bring forward, or to write, or to compose a different (ἑτέραν) faith as a rival to that established by the holy Fathers assembled with the Holy Spirit in Nicaea. But those who shall dare to compose a different faith, or to introduce or offer it to persons desiring to turn to the acknowledgment of the truth, whether from

3. Council of Ephesus, Second Session, July 10, 431.

Heathenism or from Judaism, or from any heresy whatsoever, shall be deposed, if they be bishops or clergymen; bishops from the episcopate and clergymen from the clergy; and if they be laymen, they shall be anathematized."[4]

Elucidating this passage, St. Cyril, the Patriarch of Alexandria, who presided at the Council, was adamant. He wrote to the Patriarch John of Antioch, "We do not permit anyone in any way to upset the defined faith or the creed drawn up by the holy fathers who assembled at Nicaea as the times demanded. We give neither ourselves nor them the license to alter any expression there or to change a single syllable, remembering the words: 'Remove not the ancient landmarks which your fathers have set.'"[5]

Yet centuries after the Council of Ephesus, the Roman Church did alter an expression and change more than a syllable. The Creed as promulgated at the Council of Ephesus reads, "I believe in the Holy Spirit, the Lord, the Giver of Life, who proceeds from the Father." Nearly 600 years later, in 1014, Pope Benedict VIII altered the Creed as recited in the Roman Catholic Mass to say, "Who proceeds from the Father and the Son" ("and the Son" in Latin is *filioque*).

This change was centuries in the making, and many popes had resisted it. Once the change was made, defenders of papal infallibility argued that the Filioque had not violated the canon of the Council of Ephesus because it did not teach "a different faith" from the one that the Council taught. It merely elucidated a controverted point. St. Cyril's warning not to "change a single syllable" was, they argue—although Cyril was a great saint, a Father of the Church, and one of the most important theologians of the early centuries of the Church—merely a theological opinion, not a dogma.

The matter of the Filioque and the change to the Nicene Creed is beyond the scope of this discussion. Regarding the question of whether or not the Pope had the authority to add it to the Creed, the case of Pope Leo III is noteworthy. Among the Popes who opposed the introduction of the Filioque into the Creed

4. Council of Ephesus, Seventh Session, Canon VII.
5. St. Cyril of Alexandria, Letter of Cyril to John of Antioch about peace, in Decrees of the Ecumenical Councils Volume One Nicaea I to Lateran V, Norman P. Tanner, S.J., editor, Sheed & Ward and Georgetown University Press, 1990, p. 73.

before Benedict VIII, Leo III's opposition was the most emphatic. He clearly did not see himself as authorized to add the phrase to the statement of Faith, regardless of whether or not it was in harmony with the existing Creed or within the scope of his authority as he saw it to do so.

Leo had crowned the Frankish king Charlemagne Holy Roman Emperor in 800, and Charlemagne was a strong proponent of the Filioque, which he saw as a safeguard against heretics in the West who were denying that the Son was equal to the Father. Charlemagne lobbied hard for the addition to the Creed; in response, Pope Leo publicly declared his opposition to this clause by having the Creed without the Filioque posted prominently on silver plates in St. Peter's Basilica. Said Leo of the plates, "I, Leo, put these here for the love and protection of the Orthodox faith."[6] He noted that the Ecumenical Councils that had formulated the Creed, "acted upon divine illumination rather than by human wisdom...and far be it from me to count myself their equal."[7] Pope Leo III apparently did not hold to the later papal view that popes are above Ecumenical Councils.

Quite aside from the question of whether or not the Filioque is in harmony with the Orthodox understanding of the Procession of the Holy Spirit, Pope Leo's plates create several problems for defenders of papal infallibility. Clearly, the question of the procession of the Holy Spirit is a matter of faith, and if the Creed is not, in essence, a definition of dogma, then nothing is. But Pope Leo III declared definitively that the Creed should not contain the Filioque, and Pope Benedict VIII added it. Either one of them could be infallible, or neither were, but they both couldn't be.

The usual objection made at this point in the argument is that Pope Leo was not speaking *ex cathedra*; that is, he was not intending with his silver plates to define the exact parameters of the Creed and definitively rule out the Filioque. But when the Pope of Rome has the Creed as he has received it engraved and publicly posted, what is he conceivably doing other than intending to define a matter of faith? Here again, if papal infallibility is to be defined so narrowly as

6. Johann Jakob Herzog, Real-encyclopädie für protestantische Theologie und Kirche, Volume 8, Rudolf Peffer, 1857, p. 314.

7. Ratio de symbol fidei inter Leonem III papam et missos Caroli imperatoris, in Siecienski, p. 217.

to be considered not in play in instances such as this one, it is essentially a dead letter. If, on the other hand, Pope Leo's plates did fall within the scope of papal infallibility, then Benedict VIII was contravening the faith.

It does appear as if Pope Benedict VIII violated the canon of the Council of Ephesus that forbade the promulgation of any other Creed, and Pope Leo III would have been among the first to say so.

The addition to the Creed that Pope Benedict made also took for granted the proposition that the pope had the authority to make such judgments of himself, without the consultation and deliberation of an ecumenical council, and that his judgment would be final. Pope Benedict VIII may have thought that in the early part of the eleventh century, but none of his predecessors did, and such an idea had never been enunciated at an ecumenical council. Pope Benedict's assertiveness would likely have surprised his predecessors, Pope Celestine and Pope Leo I, both of whom submitted their dogmatic statements for the approval of ecumenical councils.

THE COUNCIL OF CHALCEDON

Much the same can be said of the Fourth Ecumenical Council, held in Chalcedon, near Constantinople, in 451: the Fathers examined a papal document and found it orthodox; they did not simply accept it as the infallible judgment of Christ's Vicar. The See of Rome was certainly recognized as the first See in the Church. But Roman Catholic apologists all too often take affirmations that the pope is the successor of St. Peter and that he has the primacy as meaning that he has a jurisdiction that is "ordinary and immediate, both over each and all the Churches and over each and all the Pastors and the faithful," as Vatican I avows, and is infallible when defining dogmas of faith and morals.[8]

This was clearly not what was meant by the Roman primacy before the Great Schism. The pope was the first bishop in the Church, in the sense that his was the final court of appeal in disputes between bishops, such as questions as to who was the rightful occupant of a particular bishopric; however, dogmatic disputes were settled not by the pope, but by ecumenical councils, which

---

8. Pastor Aeternus III.

examined his statements for orthodoxy. The pope also did not exercise any ordinary or immediate authority over the bishops, pastors, or faithful in the East.

And so before the Council of Chalcedon, Pope Leo wrote a document, known as the *Tome*, setting forth the orthodox position on the question of Christ's natures: that He has two natures, a divine and a human nature, in one divine Person. Cecropius, Bishop of Sebastopol, said at the Council that, "The most holy Archbishop of Rome has given a formula with which we agree, and we have all subscribed his letter." His statement assumes the possibility that the Fathers, or some group of them, might not have agreed.

Anatolius, Patriarch of Constantinople, declared, "The letter of the most holy and religious Archbishop Leo agrees with the creed of our 318 Fathers at Nice [Nicaea], and of the 150 who afterwards assembled at Constantinople, and confirmed the same faith, and with the proceedings at Ephesus under the most blessed Cyril, who is among the saints, by the Ecumenical and holy Council, when it condemned Nestorius. I therefore agree to it, and willingly subscribe to it."[9] These words show that Anatolius studied the *Tome* carefully before declaring it as orthodox, instead of simply receiving it as the final judgment of the one who was the final arbiter of what constituted orthodoxy.

When the *Tome* was read out at the Council, the Fathers once again erupted into pious exclamations, as they had at Ephesus, "This is the faith of the fathers; this is the faith of the apostles. So we all believe; so the Orthodox believe. Anathema to him who does not so believe. Peter has spoken these things through Leo. So taught the apostles. Piously and truly did Leo teach; so taught Cyril; the eternal memory of Cyril! Leo and Cyril taught the same; anathema to him who does not so believe! This is the true faith. So think the Orthodox. This is the faith of the fathers."[10]

The same question arises as at Ephesus: why was the Fathers' approval necessary? Why did they need to affirm that Leo's letter was orthodox? Why did they affirm that Leo's teaching was the same as that of St. Cyril,

9. Henry Wace, A Select Library of Nicene and Post-Nicene Fathers of the Christian Church, Second Series, Volume 14, Christian literature Company, 1900, p. 244.

10. Council of Chalcedon, Second Session, October 10, 451.

the Patriarch of Alexandria, who had died several years before? Imagine the bishops of Vatican II exclaiming that the teaching of Pope John XXIII or Paul VI coincided with that of the Archbishop of Paris or Milan: it would have been seen as an incongruous and unnecessary affirmation.

Canon 9 of the Council stipulates, "If a bishop or a cleric is in dispute with the metropolitan of the same province, let him engage either the Exarch of the Diocese or the See of imperial Constantinople, and let him bring his case before him."[11] Likewise, Canon 17 states: "And if anyone be wronged by his metropolitan, let the matter be decided by the Exarch of the Diocese or by the throne of Constantinople, as aforesaid."[12] No mention is made of appealing to Rome, even though the same council notes that Rome has the primacy.

These canons appear to establish the Church of Constantinople as a court of appeal for the Eastern Churches, while Rome was already recognized as such in the West. This, too, does not jive with the contemporary reality of Roman Catholicism. While sometimes cardinal bishops of major cities achieve prominence, there is no court of appeal for disputes other than Rome. The very idea that there could be one would be contrary to the Pope's full, ordinary, universal, and immediate jurisdiction; when one bishop of the Church possesses that, why would there possibly be need of any other place to which disputed issues could be taken? But the fact that the Council stipulated this for Constantinople in two canons, and Rome did not object, indicates that there was no understanding on anyone's part at that time that the Pope had, or should have, that kind of authority.

---

11. Council of Chalcedon, Canon 9.
12. Council of Chalcedon, Canon 17.

In Canon 28, the Council of Chalcedon decreed:

> Following in all things the decisions of the holy Fathers,
> and acknowledging the canon, which has been just read, of
> the One Hundred and Fifty Bishops beloved-of-God (who
> assembled in the imperial city of Constantinople, which
> is New Rome, in the time of the Emperor Theodosius of
> happy memory), we also do enact and decree the same
> things concerning the privileges of the most holy Church
> of Constantinople, which is New Rome. For the Fathers
> rightly granted privileges to the throne of old Rome, because
> it was the royal city. And the One Hundred and Fifty most
> religious Bishops, actuated by the same consideration, gave
> equal privileges to the most holy throne of New Rome, justly
> judging that the city which is honored with the Sovereignty
> and the Senate, and enjoys equal privileges with the old
> imperial Rome, should in ecclesiastical matters also be
> magnified as she is, and rank next after her...

Note that the authority of Rome is recognized as stemming not from
the pope being the successor of St. Peter, but "because it was the royal city."
Rome's importance in the Church, according to the Fathers of Chalcedon,
was a result of its importance in the world. And now that Constantinople was
"the city which is honored with the Sovereignty and the Senate," it was to have
"equal privileges with the old imperial Rome, should in ecclesiastical matters
also be magnified as she is, and rank next after her."

It would have been inconceivable for the Fathers of Chalcedon to have
decreed this if they believed that the Pope of Rome possessed full power
over the Church by virtue of being the successor of St. Peter; if that was so,
how could they possibly grant "equal privileges" to another See that did not
enjoy the succession from St. Peter? The Fathers of Chalcedon clearly did
believe that the pope was the successor of St. Peter; they say so. But it is just
as clear that they did not invest that succession with the significance it is given
in the Roman Catholic theology articulated at Vatican I and Vatican II. They

thought the pope's primacy in the Church stemmed from the greatness of his city, and thus reasoned that they could place Constantinople on an equal footing with Rome since it had replaced Rome as the capital of the Empire.

Pope Leo rejected Canon 28. But even as he did so, Leo demonstrated that he, too, understood that the status of the churches was based on the ecclesiastical canons, not on divine right. Writing to the Emperor Marcian on May 22, 452, Leo strongly protests against Canon 28, but never mentions the Apostle Peter or argues that Constantinople cannot be given equal privileges with Rome because St. Peter alone was given the primacy and full, ordinary, and immediate jurisdiction over the Church. Wrote Leo:

> Let the city of Constantinople have, as we desire, its high rank, and under the protection of God's right hand, long enjoy your clemency's rule. Yet things secular stand on a different basis from things divine: and there can be no sure building save on that rock which the Lord has laid for a foundation.

One might expect after saying this that Pope Leo would start discussing the prerogatives of St. Peter, but instead, he invokes the earlier ecumenical councils, arguing that their decisions cannot be changed:

> He that covets what is not his due, loses what is his own. Let it be enough for Anatolius that by the aid of your piety and by my favor and approval he has obtained the bishopric of so great a city. Let him not disdain a city which is loyal, though he cannot make it an Apostolic See; and let him on no account hope that he can rise by doing injury to others.

St. Andrew the First-Called, the brother of St. Peter, is traditionally regarded as the founder of the Church in Byzantium, which became Constantinople; Pope Leo was either unaware of this or professing to be. But what he is arguing here is that Constantinople cannot be given a rank above Alexandria and Antioch, which before Chalcedon were the second and third Sees in the Church; as they were Apostolic Sees, founded by St. Mark and

St. Peter, respectively, and so a See that was not founded by an apostle, as Leo was claiming of Constantinople, could not have a status above theirs. Leo invokes not Petrine privilege, but the First Council of Nicaea:

> For the privileges of the churches determined by the canons of the holy Fathers, and fixed by the decrees of the Nicene Synod, cannot be overthrown by any unscrupulous act, nor disturbed by any innovation. And in the faithful execution of this task by the aid of Christ I am bound to display an unflinching devotion; for it is a charge entrusted to me, and it tends to my condemnation if the rules sanctioned by the Fathers and drawn up under the guidance of God's Spirit at the Synod of Nicaea for the government of the whole Church are violated with my connivance (which God forbid), and if the wishes of a single brother have more weight with me than the common good of the Lord's whole house.

The controversy between the East and the West over papal authority generally featured the papal party arguing that the pope had authority over the entire Church by divine appointment, and the opposition maintaining that the Roman primacy was instead established by the ecclesiastical canons. Pope Leo, in stating that the See of Constantinople not be elevated to equal status with that of Rome, argued like an Easterner, on the basis of the canons, not by invoking the status of the Popes as Roman Catholics later came to see it.

POPE VIGILIUS

The Fifth Ecumenical Council, held in Constantinople in 553, condemned three writings that reflected the doctrine of the Nestorian heresy: those of Theodore of Mopsuestia; some of the writings of Theodoret of Cyrus; and the letter of Ibas of Edessa to Maris. Collectively these were known as the Three Chapters. Pope Vigilius, however, refused to join in the condemnation.

This annoyed the Emperor Justinian considerably, as he wanted the condemnation of the Three Chapters to try to reconcile another heretical group, the Monophysites, to the Church. The Monophysites falsely claimed that the doctrine of the Council of Chalcedon was Nestorian, so the Council and the Emperor, in condemning the Three Chapters, were clarifying the distinction between Orthodoxy and Nestorianism.

The Catholic Encyclopedia of 1913 explains that Vigilius, after maintaining his refusal to condemn the Three Chapters, "seems to have been banished..."[13] Even worse, "Already in the seventh session of the council Justinian caused the name of Vigilius to be stricken from the diptychs, without prejudice, however, it was said, to communion with the Apostolic See."[14] This meant in effect that the Council had deposed the pope. Finally Vigilius was recalled from exile and allowed to return to Rome after recognizing the Fifth Ecumenical Council and condemning the Three Chapters.

Throughout this entire controversy, no one seems to have objected that it was impossible or unlawful for an Ecumenical Council to depose the Supreme Pontiff. The Council's authority to do so seems to have been generally accepted.

---

13. "Second Council of Constantinople," Catholic Encyclopedia, 1913.
14. Ibid.

Pope Gregory the Great, Dialogist

CHAPTER FIVE

Pope Gregory the Great and Pope Honorius

POPE GREGORY THE GREAT

In 586, the Byzantine Emperor Maurice conferred the title "Ecumenical" on Patriarch St. John the Faster of Constantinople, and Pope St. Gregory the Great was alarmed. The title simply meant that John was Patriarch of the imperial city, but Gregory took it as meaning that John was proclaiming himself to be the universal bishop of the entire Church.

Modern-day Roman Catholics might have expected Gregory to write to John and say that the pope alone was the universal bishop, and that there was no room in the Church for another. Instead, however, Gregory told John that the title itself was illegitimate because there was no universal bishop, "Whoever calls himself universal bishop, or desires this title, is, by his pride, the precursor to the Antichrist."[1]

How could Gregory possibly have written this if he believed that as pope, he had, as Vatican I says, "superiority of ordinary power over all other Churches, and that this power of jurisdiction of the Roman Pontiff, which is truly episcopal, is immediate," and that the Roman Pontiff possesses the "supreme power" of "governing the Universal Church"?[2] Clearly, Gregory the Great disagreed with his eleventh-century successor, Pope Gregory VII, who wrote: "The Roman Pontiff alone can with right be called universal."

---

1. Epistle of Pope St. Gregory I to St. John the Faster.
2. Pastor Aeternus, I, III.

Defenders of the idea that the Pope has universal jurisdiction have pointed out that Gregory the Great also wrote, "As to what they say of the Church of Constantinople, who doubts that it is subject to the Apostolic See? This is constantly owned by the most pious Emperor and by our brother and Bishop of that city." And also, "If any fault is found among bishops, I know not any one who is not subject to it (the Apostolic See); but when no fault requires otherwise, all are equal according to the estimation of humility."

However, the primacy of the pope, as being the first bishop in the Church at that time, is not what is at issue. The question is whether that primacy conferred ordinary and universal jurisdiction over the entire Church, as well as infallibility when defining doctrines of faith and morals. Often Roman Catholic apologists produce evidence that the pope had the primacy in the first millennium as if that in itself established his universal jurisdiction and infallibility, but it is clear that no one—no one—in the first millennium believed that universal jurisdiction and infallibility were components of infallibility. And Gregory the Great clearly rejected the idea that any bishop had universal jurisdiction.

Gregory the Great also wrote this to John:

> What will you say to Christ, Who is the Head of the universal Church—what will you say to Him at the last judgment—you, who by your title of universal, would bring all His members into subjection to yourself? Whom I pray you tell me, whom do you imitate by this perverse title if not Lucifer who, despising the legions of angels, his companions, endeavored to mount to the highest?... But if anyone usurp in the Church a title which embraces all the faithful, the universal Church—O blasphemy!— will then fall with him, since he makes himself to be called the universal. May all Christians reject this blasphemous title—this title which takes the sacerdotal honor from every priest the moment it is insanely usurped by one.[3]

On the basis of this, some Roman Catholic apologists have argued that Gregory thought that John had, by accepting the title "universal bishop," had

---

3. Pope Gregory the Great, Letter to John, Bishop of Constantinople.

effectively proclaimed himself the *sole* bishop, deposing all others. But as John had done no such thing, it is extremely unlikely that Gregory actually meant that he had stripped "the sacerdotal honor from every priest" in any literal fashion. Clearly, Pope Gregory meant that if there was a universal bishop, then all other bishops were not really bishops in their own right anymore, but were mere suffragans, assistants, or surrogates of the universal bishop. And indeed, Gregory's words proved prophetic: Roman Catholic bishops today do not behave the way bishops of the first millennium did, taking an active role in the determination of theological disputes and contributing to the theological wealth of the Church, after the manner of St. Athanasius, St. Basil the Great, St. John Chrysostom, St. Cyril of Alexandria, and so many others. Instead, they look to Rome on such matters and are executors of the pope's wishes in their localities. Pope Gregory's warning to the Ecumenical Patriarch proved true—of Roman Catholic bishops under the authority of the universal bishop in Rome.

In any case, there is a clear divergence between Pope Gregory I—"Whoever calls himself universal bishop, or desires this title, is, by his pride, the precursor to the Antichrist"—and Pope Gregory VII—"The Roman Pontiff alone can with right be called universal." One of these statements may be an accurate summation of one aspect of the faith of the apostles, the Orthodox faith. But they cannot both be.

My old friend James Likoudis, the most prominent convert from Orthodoxy to Roman Catholicism and a fierce and convinced Roman Catholic apologist, also points to another statement from Gregory I, which he quotes in this way, "Who does not know that the holy Church is founded on the solidity of the Chief Apostle, whose name expressed his firmness, being called Peter from Petra (Rock)?... Though there were many Apostles, only the See of the Prince of the Apostles...received supreme authority in virtue of its very principate." (Letter to the Patriarch Eulogius of Alexandria, Ep. 7)[4]

I know James Likoudis is an honest and honorable man, and thus I am sure that he did not leave the material in the last ellipses out of his quotation in order to mislead. Perhaps he thought that the omitted statement would

---

4. Thomas Seraphim Hamilton, "Gregory the Great: Defender of Papal Supremacy?," Orthodox Christianity, July 26, 2012. https://www.orthodox-christianity.com/2012/07/pope-st-gregory-the-great-defender-of-papal-supremacy/

confuse the reader and require eludication that would take him far from his main argument. In any case, the full quotation reads this way, "Though there were many Apostles, only the See of the Prince of the Apostles, *which is the See of one in three places, received supreme authority in virtue of its very principate*" (emphasis added).[5]

"The See of one in three places." St. Gregory is referring to the fact that St. Peter is regarded in Tradition as the founder of the Sees of Rome and Antioch, and his disciple St. Mark, author of the second Gospel, is the founder of the See of Alexandria. He is emphasizing the precedence of the Sees as it stood before the Council of Chalcedon and its 28th Canon, which Rome did not yet accept, and was saying the Churches of Rome, Alexandria, and Antioch all took precedence over Constantinople. He clearly believed that all three at once, together, were the See of Peter, the Prince of the Apostles, a belief that casts an intriguing light over the statements of Petrine primacy and authority from his predecessors going back to Leo the Great, and many of his successors. Just as clearly, he did not view the supreme authority of the See of the Prince of the Apostles and indicating that Rome had monarchical authority to dictate to the other Patriarchates.

Any lingering doubt that Pope Gregory rejected the very idea of a universal bishop was dispelled by Gregory himself in another context, when Eulogius, Patriarch of Alexandria, addressed him as "Universal Pope." The Patriarchs of Alexandria were and still are known as "Popes," and so Eulogius was apparently contrasting his own status as Pope of Alexandria with the Pope of Rome, who exercised power over the entire Church. But the Pope of Rome himself would have none of it. Gregory wrote to Eulogius not only rejecting the title of "Universal Pope," but the very idea that the Pope of Rome could issue commands to the other Patriarchs, something that later Popes took for granted:

> Your Blessedness has also been careful to declare that you
> do not now make use of proud titles, which have sprung from
> a root of vanity, in writing to certain persons, and you address
> me saying, *As you have commanded*. This word, *command*, I beg
> you to remove from my hearing, since I know who I am, and

5. Ibid.

who you are. For in position you are my brethren, in character my fathers. I did not, then, command, but was desirous of indicating what seemed to be profitable.

Yet I do not find that your Blessedness has been willing to remember perfectly this very thing that I brought to your recollection.[6]

Pope Gregory then turned his attention to the title "Universal Pope," arguing that to use it would denigrate the authority of other bishops:

For I said that neither to me nor to anyone else ought you to write anything of the kind; and lo, in the preface of the epistle which you have addressed to myself who forbade it, you have thought fit to make use of a proud appellation, calling me Universal Pope. But I beg your most sweet Holiness to do this no more, since what is given to another beyond what reason demands is subtracted from yourself. For as for me, I do not seek to be prospered by words but by my conduct. Nor do I regard that as an honour whereby I know that my brethren lose their honour. For my honour is the honour of the universal Church: my honour is the solid vigour of my brethren. Then am I truly honoured when the honour due to all and each is not denied them. For if your Holiness calls me Universal Pope, you deny that you are yourself what you call me universally. But far be this from us. Away with words that inflate vanity and wound charity.

And, indeed, in the synod of Chalcedon and afterwards by subsequent Fathers, your Holiness knows that this was offered to my predecessors. And yet not one of them would ever use

---

6. Pope Gregory the Great, Epistle XXX, To Eulogius, Bishop of Alexandria, 241b. https://www.ccel.org/ccel/schaff/npnf212.iii.v.viii.xviii.html#fnf_iii.v.viii.xviii-p9.1

this title, that, while regarding the honour of all priests in this world, they might keep their own before Almighty God.[7]

So according to Pope Gregory, several Popes rejected a title that later Popes claimed for themselves and demanded that others accord to them.

POPE HONORIUS

The Council of Chalcedon did not, unfortunately, put an end to the controversies that roiled the Church about the natures of Christ. Those who held the doctrine that Christ had a single divine nature into which His human nature was subsumed went into schism; this was a considerable part of the Church of the day, including a great part of the Churches of Egypt and Syria. In the seventh century, Patriarch Sergius of Constantinople and several other clerics tried to heal this schism with a compromise formula, teaching that Christ had only one will.

However, St. Sophronius, Patriarch of Jerusalem, stoutly opposed this, arguing that to say that Christ had two wills was part and parcel of saying that He had a divine and a human nature; to deny that He had a human will meant that He didn't really have a human nature at all. Sophronius rightly argued that Monothelitism, the idea that Christ had only one will, was as much a heresy as Monophysitism, the doctrine that He had only one nature.

Sergius tried to enlist Pope Honorius on his side, writing to him and asking whether it was acceptable to say that Christ had only one will. The Pope responded in the affirmative, "We confess one will of our Lord Jesus Christ, since our (human) nature was plainly assumed by the Godhead, and this being faultless, as it was before the Fall."

Here again, the same arguments can be made that were made about Pope Innocent and Pope Zosimus. Yes, they did not use the 19th/20th century formula for Popes defining dogmas, but they all clearly meant to define a doctrine of faith to be held by the whole Church. Pope Honorius' statement comes in a letter to Sergius, who was Ecumenical Patriarch of Constantinople,

---

7. Pope Gregory the Great, Epistle XXX, To Eulogius, Bishop of Alexandria, 241b. https://www. ccel.org/ccel/schaff/npnf212.iii.v.viii.xviii.html#fnf_iii.v.viii.xviii-p9.1

in response to the Ecumenical Patriarch's doctrinal question. It was not, therefore, simply Honorius' private opinion.

And it was heresy. Some have argued that Honorius' statement that there was "one will of our Lord Jesus Christ" was tantamount to the modern expression "one mind": to say "we are of one mind on this matter" means that we agree, not that our two heads share a single brain, and that thus Honorius was saying that the Lord had "one will" because His human will always agreed with His divine will.

However, given the condemnation of Pope Honorius by the Holy Fathers, to speculate at such a long distance about his intentions is to go down a dangerous road. Also, this argument doesn't actually exonerate the Pope. He was writing about a controverted issue at a time when the formula he endorsed was being used by heretics in order to further their heresy, and he effectively placed his stamp of approval upon their doing so. The Monothelites could and did maintain that the Pope himself had confessed "one will of our Lord Jesus Christ," and was therefore of their party.

So the pope, if he was not strictly speaking guilty of heresy, was undeniably guilty of endorsing a heretical formula and thereby allowing heresy to spread instead of identifying it and combating it. Accordingly, he was condemned after his death by the Sixth Ecumenical Council, the Third Council of Constantinople in 680. Pope Agatho declared in letters to the emperor and the Council that, "the evangelical and apostolic uprightness of the Orthodox faith" was "established upon the firm rock of this Church of blessed Peter, the Prince of the Apostles, which by his grace and guardianship remains free from all error."[8]

In an implicit rejection of this claim, however, the Fathers of that Council condemned Honorius, "who was some time Pope of the Elder Rome," for "raising up for the whole Church the stumbling-blocks of one will and one operation in the two natures of Christ our true God, one of the Holy Trinity."[9] Accordingly, "we define that there shall be expelled from the holy Church of God and anathematized Honorius who was some time Pope of

8. The Letter of Agatho, Pope of Old Rome, to the Emperor, and the Letter of Agatho and of 125 Bishops of the Roman Synod, Addressed to the Sixth Council.
9. Third Ecumenical Council of Constantinople, Definition of Faith.

Old Rome, because of what we found written by him to Sergius, that in all respects he followed his view and confirmed his impious doctrines."[10] The Council Fathers exclaimed, "To Honorius, the heretic, anathema!"[11]

The seventeenth-century French bishop and theologian Jacques-Bénigne Bossuet held this to be, "a certain proof that they did not understand Agatho's expressions as if it were necessary to receive without discussion every decree of Roman Pontiffs even *de fide*, inasmuch as they are subjected to the supreme and final examination of a General Council."[12]

The papal legates who were present at the Council raised not one word of protest against all this. Pope Leo II, in confirming the Council's decrees, wrote, "We anathematize the inventors of the new error, that is, Theodore, Sergius... and also Honorius, who did not attempt to sanctify this Apostolic Church with the teaching of Apostolic tradition, but by profane treachery permitted its purity to be polluted."[13] Leo wrote to the Spanish bishops that Honorius, "did not, as became the Apostolic authority, extinguish the flame of heretical teaching in its first beginning, but fostered it by his negligence."[14]

Pope Honorius was subsequently condemned by the Seventh Ecumenical Council in 787; Rome did not protest. Likewise, according to the Catholic Encyclopedia of 1913, he was condemned in, "the oath taken by every new pope from the eighth century to the eleventh in the following words: 'Together with Honorius, who added fuel to their wicked assertions' (*Liber diurnus*, ii, 9)....The condemnation of Pope Honorius was retained in the lessons of the Breviary for 28 June (St. Leo II) until the eighteenth century."[15]

There is a great deal of controversy among opponents and defenders of the doctrine of papal infallibility over whether or not Honorius was condemned by the popes for heresy or simply for neglecting to defend the Orthodox faith, and over whether or not he was speaking *ex cathedra*. The

---

10. Third Ecumenical Council of Constantinople, Session XIII, The Sentence Against the Monothelites.
11. Third Ecumenical Council of Constantinople, Session XVI, Extracts from the Acts.
12. Jacques-Bénigne Bossuet, Défense de la Tradition et des Saints Pères, lib. VII., cap. xxiv.
13. Pope Leo II, Letter to Emperor Constantine IV, May 7, 683.
14. "Pope Honorius I," Catholic Encyclopedia, 1913.
15. Ibid.

most important aspect of the condemnation of Honorius, however, is that two Ecumenical Councils and numerous popes for several centuries would dare to condemn the pope at all. If a pope today approved of a heretical formula that had not yet explicitly been defined as a heresy by an Ecumenical Council or previous popes, it would become the new orthodoxy among Roman Catholics; no subsequent Roman Catholic council would dare to condemn it or the pope who endorsed it. The very fact that Pope Honorius was condemned by the Third Council of Constantinople, and that popes accepted that condemnation, even with reservations, indicates that no one in the Church in those days thought that *Roma locuta, causa finita est.* For Rome had spoken on Monothelitism in Pope Honorius' letter to Sergius, and yet the question remained very much alive.

From the Monastery of St. Stephen at Meteora, Greece

The 8th Ecumenical Council

CHAPTER SIX

Saint Photios, the Great Schism, and Beyond

St. Photios

According to the historian Francis Dvornik, "Few names in the history of Christianity have inspired feelings so conflicting as that of the Greek Patriarch Photios. Saint and hero in the eyes of the Christian East, he is branded by the Christian West as the man who unbolted the safeguards of unity and let loose the disruptive forces of dissent and schism."[1] The ninth-century schism between the Churches of Rome and Constantinople that bears his name hinged upon many of the issues that were also involved in the Great Schism of two centuries later, which has never been healed. A closer look at what came to be known as the "Photian Schism," however, reveals a way forward toward a genuine reconciliation of the Churches, one offered by St. Photios himself.

The Photian Schism was precipitated by a complicated series of events involving Photios' predecessor as Ecumenical Patriarch, St. Ignatios, and Pope Nicholas of Rome. The controversies primarily involved two issues of jurisdiction: whether the new Church of Bulgaria fell within the realm of Rome or of Constantinople, and whether the Pope of Rome had the right to intervene in the internal affairs of the Church of Constantinople. When the Byzantine Emperor deposed St. Ignatios in favor of St. Photios, Pope

---

1. Francis Dvornik, The Photian Schism: History and Legend, Cambridge University Press, 1948, p. 1.

Nicholas sent legates to investigate the legitimacy of what had been done, deeply offending those in the Eastern Church who believed that their internal affairs were theirs and theirs alone to manage.

The pope justified his intervention with a resounding assertion of his own prerogatives. The Bishop of Rome, he wrote, was, "ruler of the whole world," with authority, "built on Blessed Peter by the word of Christ, deposited in the Church herself, observed in ancient times and celebrated by the sacred universal Synods, and venerated jointly by the entire Church... granted to this holy Church by Christ, not given by synod."[2] He wrote a lengthy letter to the Bulgarians, enjoining upon them the correctness of various Roman practices over Byzantine usage, and arguing that, "the blessed Peter, who lives and presides in his see, offers the truth of the faith to those who seek it. Indeed, the holy Roman Church has always been without spot or wrinkle, obviously because it was established by the man whose confession of faith was divinely approved."[3]

In a council held in Rome in 863, Nicholas declared that St. Photios was to be deposed, along with all the clergy he had ordained. Yet in Constantinople, the pope's decrees were simply ignored, which would have been unthinkable if it had been taken for granted that the Bishop of Rome had ordinary and universal jurisdiction over the whole Church. The Ecumenical Patriarchate sent no response to Rome at all.[4]

As the key issues remained controverted, however, in 866 St. Photios addressed an encyclical to the Eastern Patriarchs, arguing in turn for Byzantine practices over those of the Church of Rome on issues of fasting and the like. He devoted most of this Encyclical to criticism of the Filioque, charging that the Westerners "attempted by their false opinions and distorted words to ruin the holy and sacred Nicene Symbol of Faith—which by both synodal and universal decisions possesses invincible power—by adding to it that the Holy

2. Pope Nicholas I, Epistula 88 ad Michaelum Imperatorem, in A. Edward Siecienski, The Papacy and the Orthodox: Sources and History of a Debate, Oxford University Press, 2017, p. 221.
3. Pope Nicholas I, Epistula 99 Responsa Nicholai ad consulta Bulgarorum, in Siecienski, p. 221.
4. David Ford, "St. Photios the Great, the Photian Council, and Relations with the Roman Church," Pravoslavie.ru, October 18, 2016.

Spirit proceeds not only from the Father, as the Symbol declares, but from the Son also. Until now, no one has ever heard even a heretic pronounce such a teaching. What Christian can accept the introduction of two sources into the Holy Trinity; that is, that the Father is one source of the Son and the Holy Spirit, and that the Son is another source of the Holy Spirit, thereby transforming the monarchy of the Holy Trinity into a dual divinity?" [5]

St. Photios added, "Nevertheless, even if we did not cite all these and other innovations of the Church of Rome, the mere citing of their addition of the Filioque to the Nicene Creed would be enough to subject them to a thousand anathemas. This innovation blasphemes the Holy Spirit, or more correctly, the entire Holy Trinity."[6] He clearly believed, and assumed that those who read his encyclical would believe, that the Pope of Rome could err on matters of faith. He doesn't attempt to refute claims of papal infallibility because such claims were virtually unknown at the time.

St. Photios' statement that the Nicene Creed in its original formulation "by both synodal and universal decisions possesses invincible power" is apparently a reference to the statement of the Council of Ephesus that the wording of the Creed cannot be changed. He also declared, "From the Italian region, we have received a synodal letter citing many grave matters against the Bishop of Old Rome. Accordingly, the Orthodox there ask us to free them from his great tyranny, for in that area sacred law is being scorned and Church order trampled. We were told this earlier by monks who came to us from there, and now we have received many letters stating frightening news about

5. Patriarch Photius of Constantinople: Encyclical to the Eastern Patriarchs (866), University of Oregon, https://pages.uoregon.edu/sshoemak/324/texts/photius_encyclical.htm.
6. Ford, "St. Photios the Great."

that region and asking us to relay their message to all the bishops and to the Apostolic Patriarchs as well. For that reason, I communicate to you their request by way of this epistle. Once a holy and ecumenical Christian Synod has been assembled, it will fall upon us together to resolve all these matters with the help of God and according to the rules of previous Synods, that in so doing, a deep peace may again prevail in the Church of Christ."[7]

Notably absent from his Encyclical, however, and from St. Photios' other writings, was any denunciation of papal primacy, or even of the assertions that Pope Nicholas had made regarding the nature and extent of that authority. This obviously did not mean, of course, that St. Photios accepted the pope's assertion of the authority to judge the internal affairs of the Church of Constantinople, in particular regarding the deposition of St. Ignatios. It is clear also that it did not mean that St. Photios accepted the Filioque.

St. Photios, as he was at the center of a heated controversy that went to the heart of Roman claims regarding its authority over the whole Church, had no reason to temporize or maintain silence over his views of that authority. It is likely that, in accord with the canons of the ecumenical councils, he did not dispute the papal primacy. It is clear from his criticism of the Filioque and resistance to Rome's assertion of the authority to intervene in the dispute over the Ecumenical Patriarchate that he did not consider that primacy to involve either infallibility in matters of faith or universal ordinary jurisdiction over the entire Church.

This is akin to the status of the Ecumenical Patriarchate in the Orthodox Church today.

The Ecumenical Patriarch of Constantinople is recognized as having the primacy among the bishops, and the responsibility according to the Council of Chalcedon to adjudicate disputes between the bishops. There is, however, no suggestion that he enjoys the charism of infallibility in his doctrinal pronouncements, or that he has local jurisdiction over all dioceses everywhere.

It is also clear from the controversy of St. Photios and St. Ignatios that the popes' claims to plenary ecclesiastical authority can actually exacerbate

---

7. Ibid.

problems rather than solve them or bring peace. The papal intervention into this affair did nothing to pacify the situation, and it went on for years after the Roman intervention, which if anything, only complicated matters needlessly.

What's more, the status of the council that deposed St. Photios, which was held in Constantinople in 869 and 870, also demonstrates the problems inherent in papal authority as Roman Catholics understand it today. The Roman Catholics accept this council today as the eighth ecumenical council; however, for 200 years, Rome rejected it in favor of the council held ten years later, at which St. Photios was reinstated. In 879, Pope John VIII wrote to the latter council: "And first of all receive Photios the most amazing and most reverend High-Priest of God our Brother Patriarch and co-celebrant who is co-sharer, co-participant and inheritor of the communion which is in the Holy Church of the Romans... receive the man unpretentiously. No one should behave pretentiously [following] the unjust councils which were made against him."[8] The "unjust councils" included the one that Roman Catholics now accept as the eighth ecumenical council. John VIII wrote to St. Photios, "As for the Synod that was summoned against your Reverence we have annulled here and have completely banished, and have ejected [it from our archives], because of the other causes and because our blessed predecessor Pope Hadrian did not subscribe to it."[9] At the 879–80 council, a letter from John VIII was read that stated, "We [Pope John VIII] wish that it is declared before the Synod, that the Synod which took place against the aforementioned Patriarch Photios at the time of Hadrian, the Most holy Pope in Rome, and [the Synod] in Constantinople [869/70] should be ostracized from this present moment and be regarded as annulled and groundless, and should not be co-enumerated with any other holy Synods."[10]

If councils only have ecumenical status when Popes ratify them as such, which Popes take precedence: the ones who rejected the 869–70 council, or the ones who accepted it?

---

8. Fr. George Dion Dragas, "The 8th Ecumenical Council: Constantinople IV (879/880) and the Condemnation of the Filioque Addition and Doctrine," http://www.oodegr.com/english/dogma/synodoi/8th_Synod_Dragas.htm.

9. Ibid.

10. Ibid.

NIKETAS OF NICOMEDIA, ANSELM OF HAVELBERG, AND THE NATURE OF THE CHURCH

Were the Bishop of Rome to renounce the aspects of his claims to authority that have no basis in the teachings of the apostles, the Fathers, and the Ecumenical Councils, that is the authority he could exercise in the unified Church. The Byzantine theologian Niketas of Nicomedia made this clear in 1136, in a debate in Constantinople with Bishop Anselm of Havelberg, who was visiting the city on a diplomatic mission. After Bishop Anselm admonished Niketas that Rome was the, "mother of all churches," with whom "none should disagree," Niketas responded that he had never denied or rejected the primacy of the Roman Church, as it was, "the preeminent seat of the empire... It was named the first See, and there all the others made appeal in problematic ecclesiastical cases."[11]

However, he reminded Anselm that the pope had never been acknowledged as, "the ruler of priests, nor high priest, nor anything of the sort, rather only bishop of the first See."[12] The Second Ecumenical Council, in Constantinople in 381, had decreed that, "just as old Rome long ago held primacy in ecclesiastical cases... because of its imperial status, this younger and new Rome had primacy after it because of the dignity of empire."[13] Niketas assured Anselm that, "we would be greatly embarrassed to deny what we have before our eyes as recorded by the fathers" regarding the primacy of Rome, "but do not, like you, follow it in all things nor do I consider that I must follow it in all things."[14]

Rome, said Niketas, had illegitimately claimed, "a monarchical rule that was not her office," and was now attempting to force the Eastern Churches to accept decrees, "written without our counsel, even without our knowledge."[15] Indeed, there was no doubt that the attitude of the See of Rome toward the other apostolic and patriarchal Sees had

---

11. Anselm of Havelberg, Anticimenon: On the Unity of the Faith and the Controversies with the Greeks, in Siecienski, p. 269.

12. Ibid.

13. Ibid.

14. Ibid.

15. Ibid.

changed considerably from the days of the Council of Chalcedon, when the assembled Fathers examined Pope Leo's *Tome* to determine its orthodoxy before approving it. Niketas noted this change with regret:

> If the Roman pontiff, sitting on high on the throne of his glory
> should wish to thunder at us or cast down his commands from
> on high, and if he might want to judge, rather than to rule
> us and our churches as his own will pleases and without our
> counsel, what sort of brotherhood or fatherhood might this
> be? Who could endure this with equanimity? If we did, then
> we would rightly be called—indeed we would be—slaves, not
> sons of the Church.[16]

Niketas challenged the assertion that the Church of Rome derived the fullness of authority from its succession from St. Peter, echoing many of the Fathers of the Church when he stated that the authority was not given, "to Peter only, but to all the apostles along with Peter... nor did the Holy Spirit sent from the Lord on Pentecost... descend on Peter alone. Rather he set them all afire together. We must not attribute to Peter alone the privilege that the Lord gave to all in common."[17]

To this Anselm responded by reminding Niketas that only to Peter had the Lord given the keys to the kingdom of Heaven (Matthew 16:19) and the command to, "feed my sheep" (John 21:15-17). He argued, "Just as there is one Church, so the Church has one head, and this head is the Roman Pontiff."[18]

Anselm thus articulated a primary difference between the Orthodox Christian and Roman Catholic understandings of the nature of the Church. James Likoudis wrote to me, "The Church Christ established was established as a visible body, a visible society with a visible head in Peter, Chief and Leader of the Apostolic College. I know no visible body without a head uniting its members into one unitary body. The hundreds of Orthodox bishops do not, in fact, constitute

---

16. Ibid.
17. Ibid.
18. Ibid., p. 271.

one united Church, but 14 or more independent Churches lacking a head with a mouth to pronounce infallible truth."[19]

It makes sense. A visible body needs to have a visible head. And so Roman Catholics argue that it simply makes sense that the Church, as the one Body of Christ, has one head, the Pope of Rome, the successor of Peter.

The Orthodox, however, while believing that the Church is the one Body of Christ, understand what this means in a somewhat different manner. Both Orthodox Christians and Roman Catholics believe that the Holy Eucharist is not just bread and wine, but the Body and Blood of our Lord and Savior Jesus Christ, not endlessly multiplied and divided into sections, but the sole and whole Body of Christ in every consecrated element. In a similar way, each local church is not a segment of the Body of Christ with its head in Rome; rather, it is in itself the sole and entire Body of Christ, such that if every other church all over the world were somehow destroyed, the fullness of the Church, the Body of Christ, would still exist in the world.

This is what it truly means to be "catholic"—that is, "according to the whole" (katholou). Wherever the believers are gathered, there is the Church. Not just a segment of it, but the entire mystical body of Christ and fullness of His teaching. Thus the Orthodox Church is Catholic in the truest and fullest sense.

This is the theology of St. Ignatius of Antioch, who wrote, as we have seen, that all Christians should reverence, "the bishop as Jesus Christ."[20] Just as there are not many Eucharists, but one, there are not many Christs, but one, and that Christ comes to us in the Eucharist. So also that same Christ is the head of the Church in each individual bishop. In the same way, we have seen St. Cyprian quote the Gospel passage that Roman Catholics most frequently associate with the authority of the pope, the one in which the Lord says to St. Peter, "thou art Peter, and upon this rock I will build my church; and the gates of hell shall not prevail against it. And I will give unto thee the keys of the kingdom of heaven" (Matthew

19. James Likoudis, email to Robert Spencer, March 17, 2019.
20. St. Ignatius to the Trallians, chapter 5.

16:18-19), and argue from that passage that "the Church is settled on the bishops, and every act of the Church is regulated by these same prelates."[21]

So yes, there is one earthly head of the Church, and that one head is the successor of St. Peter—that is, those bishops of the world who hold to and teach the faith of the apostles. Disputes among the bishops are settled in gatherings of all the bishops, who speak with one voice to articulate and defend that faith.

THE ROMAN YOKE

Between the time of St. Photios and that of Niketas of Nicomedia, there was, of course, the Great Schism of 1054, which has never been healed. It was the handiwork of a Cardinal of the Roman Church, Humbert of Silva Candida, whom Pope Leo IX had sent to Constantinople to discuss the differences between the Churches with the Ecumenical Patriarch Michael I Keroularios. Just after Humbert and his associates arrived in Constantinople, the news arrived that Pope Leo had died, stripping them of any authority to carry out any discussions or negotiations on behalf of the Roman Church.

Cardinal Humbert went ahead anyway, entering the grand cathedral in Constantinople, the Hagia Sophia, on July 16, 1054, during the Divine Liturgy, proceeded to the altar, and placed upon it a notice of excommunication of the Patriarch Michael. He responded by excommunicating Humbert and those who were with him. Despite the fact that Humbert was proceeding without authority and that the Ecumenical Patriarch did not excommunicate the pope, at this point, the estrangement between the two Churches became so pronounced that the breach between them has never since been healed.

There were attempts, however. The Roman Church hosted two attempts at reunion, both of which it recognizes as ecumenical councils: in Lyon in 1274 and in Florence, which concluded in 1445. Neither, however, featured much in the way of serious discussion regarding the differences between the Church. The Pope of Rome by this point was accustomed to dictating to other prelates and expecting their obedience; the idea of the bishops of the Church having the temerity to rebuke him, as they had Pope Victor, or to

---

21. St. Cyprian, Ep. 33.

review his writings to determine their orthodoxy, as we have seen they did at the Council of Chalcedon, was long gone.

Epitomizing the entirety of the proceedings at Florence was an incident that took place shortly after the arrival of the Ecumenical Patriarch Joseph in the city. Expecting a fraternal welcome from his brother bishop, the Ecumenical Patriarch was taken aback by demands that he kiss the feet of Pope Eugenius IV. In response, the Patriarch showed the Church of Constantinople's adherence to ancient traditions and practices, as opposed to the innovations that Rome was embracing. "Whence has the pope this right?" he asked. "Which synod gave it to him? Show me from what source he derives this privilege and where it is written... If the pope wants a brotherly embrace in accordance with ancient ecclesiastical custom, I will be happy to embrace him, but if he refuses, I will abandon everything and return to Constantinople."[22]

The pope relented, and the Ecumenical Patriarch remained in Florence, but the papal high-handedness manifested itself in other ways. Nor was it new at that time. During the preparations for the Council of Lyon, one Roman Catholic actually cited this high-handedness as an obstacle to the Council's prospects for success in unifying the Churches. Humbert of Romans, a French friar who had served as Master General of the Dominican Order, wrote in 1274 that, "The Roman Church knows only how to make the yoke she has laid on men's shoulders press heavily; her extortions, her numberless legates and nuncios, and the multitude of her statutes and punishments, have deterred the Greeks from reunion."[23]

Orthodox leaders made no secret of the fact that they shared this view. Half a century after the failed reunion attempt at the Council of Lyon, the English traveler Sir John Mandeville wrote about the reaction of the Orthodox to a demand for submission that had been issued by Pope John XXII (1316–1334). They told the pope, according to Mandeville, "Your plenary power over your subjects we firmly believe; your immeasurable pride we cannot

---

22. Sylvester Syropoulos, Memoirs, 4.33, in Siecienski, p. 329.

23. Johann Jakob Ignaz von Döllinger (as Janus), The Pope and the Council, third edition, Rivingtons, 1870, p. 321.

endure, and your greed we cannot satisfy. With you is Satan, with us the Lord."[24]

POPE CELESTINE III

There was, however, a steady stream of indications that the pope's "immeasurable pride" would have been better tempered with a bit of humility. On September 5, 1234, Pope Gregory IX promulgated the Papal Bull *Rex Pacificus*, declaring that the new collection of his Decretals that had just been issued was the official code of canon law for Roman Catholics. This was the highest law for Roman Catholics, sanctioned with full approval of the pope, and yet it contained this:

> A Christian man denied Christ out of hatred for his wife and united himself to a pagan woman, with whom he procreated children. The Christian woman, who had been abandoned unto the dishonor of Jesus Christ, went into a second marriage with the assent of the Archdeacon and had children. It does not seem to us that if the first husband returns to the unity of the Church she ought to depart from the second and go back to the first, especially since she was seen to have departed from him by the judgment of the Church. And, as St. Gregory [the Great] testifies, 'the affront to the Creator dissolves the right of marriage (*solvat ius matrimonii*) for the one who is left out of hatred of the Christian faith'. (...) [Concerning this question we have] the rule and the doctrine of the Apostle, by which it is said, "If the infidel depart, let him depart. For a brother or sister is not under servitude in such cases" (1 Cor. 7:15—i.e., the Pauline Privilege), as well as the famous decree of Gregory [found in the Decretum of Gratian]: 'it is not a sin if [the spouse], having been dismissed

24. Ibid., p. 322, language modernized.

for God's sake, joins another; the departing infidel [however],
has sinned and against God and against matrimony.'[25]

This was contrary to Roman Catholic teaching regarding the indissolubility
of marriage, allowing for no remarriage while one's spouse or ex-spouse was
still living except in cases of annulment. Yet it remained part of the Roman
Catholic code of canon law for nearly seven centuries, until a new code of
canon law was promulgated in 1917. The Counter-Reformation and Roman
Catholic theologian Robert Bellarmine noted, "that this teaching of Celestine
is heretical is clear, because Innocent III (Cap. "Quanto," c. 3) taught the
contrary on Divorce and the Council of Trent also defined the same thing."

So a heresy remained in the code of canon law for nearly 700 years, and
its source was a pope. Did this not demonstrate the non-infallibility of the
pope? Bellarmine said no, for, "the whole matter was still being thought out,"
and Pope Celestine was not speaking *ex cathedra*; he merely, "responded with
what seemed more probable."

Yet this is a counsel of despair. Yes, the matter was still being thought
out, but Celestine was doing more than just giving a probable opinion, as is
evidenced by the fact that his ruling was included in the Decretals of Gregory
IX, which was the code of canon law for Roman Catholics for centuries.
Opinions don't generally get included in books that are intended to give
definitive rulings on disputed questions and to contain authoritative legal texts.

THE COUNCIL OF CONSTANCE

There are at the time of this writing two popes: Pope Francis and
the retired Pope Benedict XVI, who is known as Pope Emeritus.
This unusual situation, along with Pope Francis' many highly
publicized deviations from Roman Catholic teaching and even
Christian tradition, have led some to assert that Benedict XVI is

---

25. Decretals of Gregory IX, Lib. III, Tit. XXXII, Laudabilem, 'On the conversion of the infidels,' by Pope Celestine III.

actually the true pope.[26] The theological problems created by this possibility are obvious, and include: Which Pope is owed full submission and obedience? What should one do if the two disagree with each other on an issue that involves a matter of faith?

Roman Catholics who accept Vatican I and Vatican II would argue that the second scenario is impossible, for that is what the doctrine of infallibility means: the Lord will protect His Church from falling into error and will in such an instance, therefore, ensure that the true Pope teaches the true doctrine.

But how are the faithful to know which one is the true pope? This is not a hypothetical question. During the Western Schism, which began in 1378 and ended in 1417, there were two and then three popes, all with compelling claims to the allegiance of the faithful. In 1415, the Council of Constance, which Roman Catholics consider to be the sixteenth ecumenical council, attempted to end the schism. In doing so, it issued a decree proclaiming the supreme authority of ecumenical councils, "Legitimately assembled in the Holy Spirit, constituting a general council and representing the Catholic church militant, it has power immediately from Christ; and everyone of whatever state or dignity, even papal, is bound to obey it in those matters which pertain to the faith, the eradication of the said schism, and the general reform of the said church of God in head and members."[27]

This quickly became a dead letter, as the popes rejected it and quickly reasserted their sole authority once the schism was healed. But it stands as a compelling indication that there was even awareness in the Western Church that the prevailing model of papal authority was not adequate to deal with the challenges that the Church faced. In light of the manifest flaws in the idea of a papal monarchy, the prelates of the Council of Constance were trying to reassert an older doctrine, indeed, an apostolic one, that had served the Church so well in the first millennium.

26. Antonio Socci, The Secret of Benedict XVI: Is He Still the Pope?, Angelico Press, 2019; David Gibson, "Is Benedict XVI the REAL Pope? 4 factors fueling Vatican conspiracy theories," Washington Post, November 26, 2014.

27. Council of Constance, Haec sancta, April 6, 1415.

EASTERN CATHOLICS

The failure of the Roman Catholic concept of papal authority to be effective in actually solving dogmatic controversies within the Church is epitomized by the odd, anomalous status of Eastern Catholics, a tiny grouping which many Roman Catholics are unaware even exist.

As a Melkite Greek Catholic, I was a member of one of these groups for many years. Melkites generally adhere to the Byzantine tradition. They celebrate the Divine Liturgies of St. John Chrysostom and St. Basil the Great, and for the most part, worship and pray in the manner of the Orthodox tradition. Over the years, many Roman Catholics would enter my Melkite Greek Catholic parish and express astonishment that, in the words of one visitor, it didn't look as if it were "regular Catholic." In fact, Eastern Catholic parishes usually, but not always, are in most respects completely indistinguishable from Orthodox churches. At the same time, Eastern Catholics are in full communion with the pope, can receive communion in Roman Catholic parishes, and are in all dogmatic respects fully in accord with the teachings of Roman Catholicism.

This is, for Melkites and other Eastern Catholics, a tremendous point of pride. The Eastern Catholics are, they say, the embodiment of the undivided Church of the first millennium, the fulfillment of Pope John Paul II's desire that the Church, "breathe with her two lungs."[28] However, the Eastern Catholics are largely the products of Jesuit missionary activity in canonically Orthodox lands after the failure of several attempts at reunion councils, and they exist in a peculiar, even schizophrenic, state. In my years as a Melkite, I encountered Melkites who were firm defenders in papal authority, plenary jurisdiction, and infallibility; I also encountered other Melkites who were profoundly opposed to papal authority.

There are also Melkites who insist that they are not *Roman* Catholics: they say that *Roman* refers to liturgical usage and tradition, and thus they are *Greek* Catholics, following the liturgical and spiritual traditions of Constantinople. Those who deny that they are Roman Catholics are also generally wary of

---

28. John Paul II, Ut Unum Sint, May 25, 1995, 54.

"Latinization," the process of introducing Roman Catholic practices among Eastern Catholics, which began in earnest in tandem with the Jesuit activity that brought them into communion with Rome.

Latinization often proceeds according to the assumption that Roman Catholic practices are superior to others because of the status of the pope. After centuries of this assumption spreading among Eastern Catholics, there are Melkites who pray the Rosary and light Advent candles in the weeks leading up to Christmas. There are other Melkites who believe that to do either is to compromise their very reason for existing, that is, as an outpost of Byzantine spirituality within Roman Catholicism, and exhort other Melkites to have, in the words of the late Melkite Archbishop Joseph Tawil, "the courage to be ourselves." Some Melkites revere St. Photios and the post-Great Schism St. Gregory Palamas. In my own Melkite parish, an icon of St. Gregory Palamas was displayed on the Second Sunday of Lent, over the objections of some who thought it improper to display an icon of an Orthodox saint who did not accept papal authority.

Others, however, maintain that they certainly *are* Roman Catholics, as they are in communion with Rome, and recognize the pope's universal primacy and infallibility. They proudly adopt or continue Roman Catholic practices, as these are a sign that they are indeed in communion with the Pope of Rome.

Along with all this, the fact that many Roman Catholics themselves are unaware of the existence of Eastern Catholics and do not understand their relationship to Rome makes the question of whether or not Eastern Catholics are actually *Roman* Catholics even more confused.

In my Melkite parish also, the pastor was married. After a prohibition lasting many decades, the pope recently granted permission for the Eastern Catholics in the United States to resume practicing the Orthodox tradition of ordaining married men. This was, however, in contradiction to the sixteenth-century Council of Trent, which forbade married priests.

All this is to illustrate not just that Eastern Catholics exist in a peculiar situation of being neither fish nor fowl and have no clear identity of their own. It is primarily to demonstrate that papal authority in the case of Eastern Catholics does not solve problems but only creates new ones. Melkite Catholicism was born in 1724, when the Patriarch of Antioch,

Cyril VI Tanas, declared that he was in communion with Rome, resulting in a schism in the ancient Antiochian Patriarchate. Before this, Orthodox Christians of the Patriarchate of Antioch followed Orthodox traditions, venerated Orthodox saints, and respected Orthodox authorities. The confusion and schizophrenia among Eastern Catholics began when they entered into communion with Rome; it did not exist before then. Accepting the authority of the pope created new schisms and new theological problems and solved none at all.

MISLEADING STATEMENTS REGARDING AUTHORITY

Another massive problem that the Roman Catholic understanding of papal authority and infallibility has led to within Roman Catholicism is a vast overestimation of the nature and extent of both that authority and that infallibility. The Second Vatican Council states:

> This religious submission of mind and will must be shown in a special way to the authentic magisterium of the Roman Pontiff, even when he is not speaking *ex cathedra*; that is, it must be shown in such a way that his supreme magisterium is acknowledged with reverence, the judgments made by him are sincerely adhered to, according to his manifest mind and will. His mind and will in the matter may be known either from the character of the documents, from his frequent repetition of the same doctrine, or from his manner of speaking.[29]

In August 2016, I had a lively debate with Msgr. Stuart Swetland, president of Donnelly College in Kansas City, Kansas, on a Roman Catholic radio show.[30] We were not debating a question involving Roman Catholic belief, and the question in that debate is irrelevant to this discussion at hand, but it was one on which several recent popes have made statements. Because of

29. Lumen Gentium 25.
30. https://www.youtube.com/watch?v=TvTneiqT3kA

those statements, Msgr. Swetland argued that his position, which I believe to be false, was required for Roman Catholics to believe since several popes had stated the same things he was claiming. After the debate, Msgr. Swetland helpfully supplied me with a list of recent papal statements supporting his views; then he quoted the above passage from Vatican II's Dogmatic Constitution on the Church (*Lumen Gentium*), in order to argue that I was a, "dissenter from the papal magisterium," as Roman Catholics were required to give, "religious submission of mind and will" to these papal statements, even though they weren't about Roman Catholic faith.

Initially, I thought Msgr. Swetland's charging me with heterodoxy for rejecting papal claims about an issue that didn't involve dogmas of Roman Catholicism was absurd. I thought the case was open-and-shut: the question we were debating was not a matter of faith or morals and hence was outside the pope's purview.

However, it soon dawned on me that given the text quoted above from Vatican II, there wasn't really anything wrong with Msgr. Swetland's argument. The popes had frequently repeated the false claims that Swetland was advancing. *Lumen Gentium* gives no room to the faithful to evaluate such claims for themselves on the basis of the relevant evidence; instead, it simply commands assent to his judgments that are not spoken *ex cathedra* and are frequently repeated.

I began to realize that the problem was not just that the popes were wrong about this issue; they were also wrong about their own authority and had imposed upon the Roman Catholics a standard of assent to their teachings that necessarily entangled Catholic believers in absurdities, or else left them vulnerable to charges of being disobedient.

The Church had not always been this way. And I had an idea of when it had not been. It was time for me to come home. To Orthodoxy.

Our Lady of Vladimir

CONCLUSION

Coming Home, Finally

IS THIS WHOLE ENDEAVOR WRONG?

It is clear from all this that the pope is not infallible, and does not have universal jurisdiction over the whole Church. The Church's infallibility is not expressed in his *ex cathedra* pronouncements. Even if you do not accept that Popes Innocent, Zosimus, and Celestine III were speaking *ex cathedra* when they endorsed what Roman Catholicism otherwise affirms as heresy, there is the problem of Pope Gregory the Great's rejection of not just the title, but the idea of there being a "universal bishop." There is the clear evidence that the Fathers of the Councils of Ephesus and Chalcedon examined papal statements in order to determine their orthodoxy, rather than simply accepting them as the touchstone of Orthodoxy itself.

In light of all these considerations, I gratefully rejoined the Orthodox Church, and I submit this small offering to those who are closer to God, wiser, and more intelligent than I am, asking that they pardon its faults and accept it as one man's search for the truth. If I have committed errors of fact or reasoning, I welcome corrections and will acknowledge my errors in a public forum if it is at all possible to do so.

Many, however, will find this entire exercise distasteful. I said in the *Introduction* that I am aware that I'm out of step with the times, and I feel that keenly. For centuries theological differences were the subject of heated polemics, passionate controversies, schisms, and sometimes even wars. In that, they were not so different from other matters that caused divisions between people.

In the twentieth century, however, and particularly after the Second World War, there began a large-scale international effort to put all that aside. In the political realm, the League of Nations was formed, and then the United Nations, in an attempt to make wars a thing of the past and establish an international forum where conflicts could be resolved peacefully. The Second Vatican Council (1962-1965) was unique among Roman Catholic councils, and among those seven that are accepted as ecumenical by both Roman Catholics and Orthodox Christians, in that it focused not on what divided Christians, but what united them. There were Orthodox observers at Vatican II, and the anathemas that Cardinal Humbert and Ecumenical Patriarch Michael Keroularios had pronounced in 1054 were removed in 1964 by Pope Paul VI and the Ecumenical Patriarch Athenagoras.

The Second Vatican Council rejected the idea, popular in some circles before the Council, that, "Outside the Catholic Church there is no salvation." Vatican II taught that, "Some and even very many of the significant elements and endowments which together go to build up and give life to the Church itself, can exist outside the visible boundaries of the Catholic Church: the written word of God; the life of grace; faith, hope and charity, with the other interior gifts of the Holy Spirit, and visible elements too. All of these, which come from Christ and lead back to Christ, belong by right to the one Church of Christ."[1]

The Second Vatican Council gave tremendous impetus to the ecumenical movement, the ongoing effort to resolve the differences between the various Churches and Christian groups without the rancor and polemics that had so often marked such discussions in the past. Many, but by no means all, Orthodox have been eager participants in these endeavors, and relations between Roman Catholic and Orthodox Christian leaders, so often marked by bitterness in the past, are now in general warm and friendly. The Ecumenical Patriarch Bartholomew visited Rome in 1995 and returned in later years. Pope Francis in 2019 gave the Ecumenical Patriarch Bartholomew a reliquary containing bones of St. Peter, in a gesture of respect and reconciliation that would have been unthinkable in previous centuries.

---

1. Second Vatican Council, Unitatis Redintegratio, 3.

Meanwhile, as secularism advances and atheistic regimes have waged war against religion and been responsible for the deaths of millions of people, many Christians of all faith traditions consider it paramount to set our differences aside, without denying that they exist or glossing over them, and working together in an atmosphere of mutual respect against the evil that is advancing so confidently and aggressively in our world.

To such people, this little book may seem to be out of key with its time, or even worse, an ugly return to the bad old days of division, a rejection of the noble and good endeavors at reconciliation and tolerance. Those who think this, however, may benefit from considering the fact that ultimate reconciliation and reunion between Orthodoxy and Roman Catholicism will not be possible without some consideration of what has separated them in the first place, and that will inevitably involve each side making a full and honest statement of the case for its position.

While many people today identify discussion of what unites us as charitable and discussion of what divides us as uncharitable, this is not necessarily so. What divides us can never be overcome unless it is fully acknowledged and understood by both sides, so that areas of disagreement can be addressed with an eye toward ending that disagreement. Declining to discuss areas of disagreement only ensures that such disagreement will persist.

The exchange between Pope Pius IX and the Eastern Patriarchs in 1848 is a case in point. On January 6, 1848, Pope Pius published an Apostolic Letter, "On the Supreme Throne of Peter the Apostle," in which he called the Eastern Patriarchs to return to communion with the See of Rome. Outlining several theological and historical arguments in favor of the papal prerogatives as he understood them, the Pope concluded, "We thus exhort you, and We entreat you to return without delay—to enter into communion with the Holy See of Peter in which lies the foundation of the true Church [of] Christ as affirmed by both the tradition of your forebears and the tradition of the other ancient Fathers, as well as the very words of Our Lord Jesus Christ found in the holy Gospels and that we cited to you. For it is not, and never will be possible for those who wish to be separate from the Rock [Pierre] on which the Church was divinely built, to be in communion with the One, Holy, Catholic and Apostolic Church."[2]

In response, the Eastern Patriarchs, led by the Ecumenical Patriarch Anthimos VI of Constantinople, issued an Encyclical Letter in which they explained why they were rejecting the Pope's call, answering his arguments point-by-point and making many of the points I have made in this brief book. To the Pope's Petrine arguments, they reminded him that St. Peter had been in Antioch before Rome and that there was as a result no basis in reason or revelation to exclude Antioch from the prerogatives enjoyed by the successor of Peter as Rome understood them.

The Eastern Patriarchs concluded in words that continue to resonate today, as many elements of Roman Catholicism continue to stray farther and farther from the tradition of the Fathers of the Church, to the consternation of many faithful Roman Catholics:

> From all this, every one nourished in sound Catholic doctrine, particularly his Holiness, must draw the conclusion, how impious and anti-synodical it is to attempt the alteration of our doctrine and liturgies and other divine offices which are, and are proved to be, coeval with the preaching of Christianity: for which reason reverence was always bestowed on them, and they were confided in as pure even by the old orthodox popes themselves, to whom these things were an inheritance in common with ourselves. How becoming and holy would be the mending of the innovations, the time of whose entrance in the Church of Rome we know in each case, for our illustrious fathers have testified from time to time against each novelty. But there are other reasons which should incline his Holiness to this change. First, because those things that are ours were once venerable to the Westerns, as having the same divine offices and confessing the same creed; but the novelties were not known to our

---

2. Pope Pius IX, Apostolic Letter On the Supreme Throne of Peter the Apostle, January 6, 1848.

Fathers, nor could they be shown in the writings of the orthodox Western Fathers, nor as having their origin either in antiquity or catholicity. Moreover, neither patriarchs nor councils could then have introduced novelties amongst us because the protector of religion is the very body of the Church, even the people themselves, who desire their religious worship to be ever unchanged and of the same kind as that of their fathers.[3]

The patriarchs stated:

It is incumbent on his Holiness to show before God and man, that, as prime mover of the counsel which pleases God, so is he a willing protector of the ill-treated evangelical and synodical truth, even to the sacrifice of his own interests, according to the Prophet (Is. lx. 17), a ruler in peace and a bishop in righteousness. So be it! But until there be this desired returning of the apostate Churches to the body of the One, Holy, Catholic, and Apostolic Church, of which Christ is the Head (Eph. 4:15), and each of us 'members in particular,' all advice proceeding from them, and every officious exhortation tending to the dissolution of our pure faith handed down from the Fathers is condemned, as it ought to be, synodically, not only as suspicious and to be eschewed, but as impious and soul-destroying: and in this category, among the first we place the said Encyclical to the Easterns from Pope Pius IX, Bishop of the elder Rome.[4]

These are strong words, and the tone of both letters is sometimes jarring to modern sensibilities. But neither party had any doubt about where the other one stood, or why. If they had engaged in collaborative efforts and proclaimed their love for one another, their differences would not have been

3. Encyclical of the Eastern Patriarchs, 1848.
4. Ibid.

erased. Both sides were engaged in "speaking the truth in love" (Eph. 4:15) as they saw that truth.

Many people today, on the other hand, assume that it is impossible to maintain one's love for someone with whom one has differences while speaking truly and respectfully about those differences. Disagreement is equated with being uncharitable and agreement with being charitable, and since agreement is often difficult to attain, silence about disagreements is equated with charity. Yet in the modern age, no less august personages than several recent popes have themselves suggested that such explorations as I have engaged in here are not out of order. Pope Paul VI acknowledged in 1967 that the papacy itself had, "undoubtedly" become, "the greatest obstacle on the path of ecumenism."[5] Nearly three decades later, in 1995, Pope John Paul II invited non-Catholic Christians to help the Popes of Rome, "find a way of exercising the primacy which, while in no way renouncing what is essential to its mission, is nonetheless open to a new situation."[6] It would be impossible to fulfill Pope John Paul II's request without examining what really is essential to the papal mission, and what isn't.

There is a readily available way for the new situation that John Paul asked for to be implemented. It does not require the pope in any way to renounce what is essential to the papacy: that solution would be to return to the situation of the first millennium, when the pope did indeed have the primacy among bishops, without acting as a super-bishop above even the settled decisions of ecumenical councils. The way forward is the way back, and the way back is the way forward. The pope can once again become the first bishop, presiding in love as St. Ignatius of Antioch said of the Church of Rome, without exercising pretensions to infallibility that popes clearly do not have (as Honorius and others can bear witness) and universal jurisdiction (which no one, even Pope Gregory the Great, thought the Pope had before the Great Schism).

---

5. Siecienski, p. 7.

6. Pope John Paul II, Ut Unum Sint, Pauline Books and Media, 1995, pp.102–103, in Siecienski, p. 7.

WHAT TOOK ME SO LONG

But if all this is true, why did I leave the Orthodox Church in the first place? Why did I remain a Melkite Greek Catholic for so many years? These are fair questions, and deserve answers, although the evidence I have presented in this book stands or falls regardless of my personal situation.

The short answer is, I didn't know enough, although I thought I did. One principal reason is that while I was looking into the idea of papal authority, I did not delve into the historical issues I have outlined here. It is generally nigh-impossible to find any discussion of them in contemporary literature, apart from some discussions of some of these incidents in the writings of various modern-day Roman Catholic apologists. This is simply not an issue that is preoccupying the contemporary Orthodox Church, so it is even harder to find Orthodox responses to those Roman Catholic apologetics; these are controversies that played out 1000 years ago and more, and they simply aren't burning issues for many people now.

Now, however, because of Pope Francis' frequent controversial utterances, that is changing.

Another principal reason why I was convinced in the 1980s by arguments for papal authority was because I was thoroughly convinced by the book *An Essay on the Development of Christian Doctrine*, by the celebrated 19th century convert from Anglicanism to Roman Catholicism, John Henry Cardinal Newman. Newman argues that an infallible revelation requires an infallible interpreter; otherwise, he says, it will dissolve into a babel of conflicting interpretations and warring factions, just as we have seen with the history of Protestantism. The remedy for this was, of course, an infallible Pope.

There is a big fallacy in this argument that I overlooked at the time. To say that something is needed—a single infallible interpreter a la the pope—is not the same thing as saying that something has been given. Also, the Orthodox Church holds to the doctrine of the infallibility of the Church, but maintains that this infallibility applies to the decrees of the Ecumenical Councils.

Roman Catholics say at this point that there are many councils that have claimed the status of ecumenical, but which have not been ecumenical councils at all; Roman Catholics and Orthodox Christians can agree that the "Robber Council" held in Ephesus in 449, which declared Monophysitism the faith of the Church, was one of these. And there have been others. Roman Catholics insist that what determines whether or not a council is truly an ecumenical council is the pope's approval. This is an easy path to certainty: the popes have approved of 21 councils from Nicaea in 325 to Vatican II from 1962 to 1965, and so that's that: there have been 21 ecumenical councils. The Orthodox Church does not have such a ready mechanism to determine the ecumenicity of a council: it must express the Orthodox faith in a manner consistent with what has defined before, it must be accepted by the Church, and so on.

But the fact that the Roman Catholic ecclesiology lends itself to more ready certainties does not automatically mean that those certainties have actually been given to us by God. What's more, if a doctrinal error (that of Pope Celestine III) can be part of the code of canon law for nearly 700 years, it is entirely possible that popes could be in error about the ecumenical character of numerous councils that were convened after the seven that are accepted by both Churches as ecumenical.

The doctrinal error of Pope Celestine III is no longer in the Roman Catholic code of canon law. And that brings me to my final point.

COMING HOME

I have written this book in order to explain to my family and to friends who are concerned for my salvation that I have rejoined the Orthodox Church out of a careful new consideration of the evidence and a realization that some of what are currently, but have not always been, core doctrines of Roman Catholicism, are based on false premises. I rejoined the Orthodox Church because I realized that it is the Orthodox and Catholic Church that Christ founded.

I am not writing this with the intention of saying, "Orthodox are right, Roman Catholics are wrong, and therefore all Roman Catholics should join the Orthodox Church."

Rather, I am writing to point out that the Orthodox Church *is* the Catholic Church as it existed in the first thousand years of the Church, and as it can and should exist again, if God turns His mercy toward us and if human beings are receptive enough to His light to allow this thousand-year schism to end.

Some will find this hard to see. The Orthodox Church has been criticized for its tendency to ethnophyletism, and yet the idea that parish communities should be primarily ethnic entities in which others are not welcome has been repeatedly condemned. Meanwhile, Newman and others have criticized the Orthodox Church for its stasis: there has not been an ecumenical council since 787, and there seems to be nothing like the forthright and prophetic voice speaking out on contemporary issues that so many Roman Catholics were so proud of in Pope John Paul II. However, the Church did hold what are accepted by many Orthodox as the Eighth Ecumenical Council in 879 (with papal legates present) and the Ninth Ecumenical Council in 1341–51, which condemned heresies in the West. Moreover, truly prophetic voices were heard in saints of Pope John Paul II's day, such as St. Paisios of the Holy Mountain, St. Porphyrios of Athens, and the Holy Elder Ephraim of Arizona.

Pope Francis has cast all that in a new light. His apparent disregard for traditional tenets of the Roman Catholic faith has caused great consternation among many Roman Catholics. I hope it has also led, or will lead, to a new appreciation for the "stasis" and traditionalism of Orthodoxy. There is a great deal of confusion today about the importance of tradition in the first place. Roman Catholics often celebrate masses that feature contemporary music, and many of its churches in recent decades have been built with an eye to the latest trends in modern architecture. Many people believe that to be only fitting and proper, keeping the Church relevant to people in the contemporary world.

The value of traditional worship, however, is that it communicates the timelessness and unchanging nature of the truth and of divine revelation, which because it comes from God, cannot be altered or improved upon. Worship in the Byzantine tradition is not interested in keeping up with the times, but with communicating eternal truths. As a result, the Orthodox Church is essentially the same as it has been for many centuries. Given the fact that the primary responsibility and mission of the Church of Jesus Christ is to communicate His unchanging message to every new age, that stasis is not a vice; it's a virtue. The Orthodox Church is not in thrall to the spirit of the age. It is not full of bishops, priests and monastics who equate the unchanging Gospel with activism on various fashionable issues.

Detractors sometimes describe Orthodoxy as fossilized. In reality, it is Petrified. The Orthodox Church is what St. Peter exhorts the faithful to be, "like living stones be yourselves built into a spiritual house, to be a holy priesthood, to offer spiritual sacrifices acceptable to God through Jesus Christ" (I Peter 2:5). Many have tended to emphasize the "living" aspect of this phrase without any thought about the significance of the word "stones." Like "living stones," Orthodoxy is unchanging, moving through time while holding fast to tradition not because it is dead, but because it recognizes that tradition as coming from the Lord Jesus Christ.

The fifth-century St. Vincent of Lerins stated, "That whether I or anyone else should wish to detect the frauds and avoid the snares of heretics as they rise, and to continue sound and complete in the Catholic faith, we must, the Lord helping, fortify our own belief in two ways; first, by the authority of the Divine Law, and then, by the Tradition of the Catholic Church."[7] That tradition lives on in Orthodoxy, while contemporary Roman Catholicism differs considerably from that tradition, with the discrepancies explained away by recourse to the idea of the development of doctrine. This has the unfortunate effect of diverting people who are seeking an authentic experience of Christianity.

---

7. St. Vincent of Lerins, "For the Antiquity and Universality of the Catholic Faith Against the Profane Novelties of All Heresies," II.4.

Yes, the Orthodox Church today does not have a single figure with a powerful prophetic voice, a la John Paul II, although that is as much a function of media attention as it is of the fact that no one in the Orthodox Church has the role that the pope plays in Roman Catholicism. The Orthodox Church is filled with many great saints, many holy people who are affecting positive change around the world. They do not have the popes' international media platform, but that is the very nature of the case: Orthodoxy, like the Church of the first millennium, does not have that kind of centralized authority, that single spokesman. At the same time, the Orthodox Church does not have a single figure who is confusing and demoralizing many of the faithful with his evident disregard for the traditional faith in many areas, a la Pope Francis.

So one possible way forward would be the way of the Incarnate Lord, extreme humility. For Roman Catholics to return to what it once was will require humility, and humility is one of the most important, indeed, the most important of all virtues. Roman Catholicism today is suffering from deep crises of authority and identity. Many of these problems stem from authoritative pronouncements by pope and councils that Roman Catholicism recognizes as ecumenical, but which depart from the Catholic and Orthodox faith as it was defined in the Seven Ecumenical Councils.

The humility is not needed only on one side. Were Roman Catholics to renounce the statements of Vatican I and Vatican II on papal infallibility and other doctrines that depart from the Holy Orthodoxy shared by both the Churches of Rome and Constantinople in the first millennium, and were it to return to communion with the Orthodox Church, the Ecumenical Patriarch of Constantinople would cease to be the, "first among equals," the first bishop of the Church, as he has been since the Great Schism.

As God does indeed write straight with crooked lines, I dare to hope that the ongoing assaults on Christians of all faith traditions will inspire in all Christian leaders a sense of the necessity of our unity, and the humility that would be required to reattain it.

When one looks at the Church of the first millennium, one sees an assembly of local Churches under the unifying authority of bishops, who were themselves under the authority of metropolitans and ultimately the five patriarchates of the early Church, Rome, Constantinople, Alexandria,

Antioch, and Jerusalem. None of these patriarchs were considered infallible or to have universal jurisdiction. Great doctrinal issues were settled in ecumenical councils; other issues were resolved in local councils. There was no episcopal monarchy.

When one looks at what is presented as Christianity today, the Orthodox Church alone operates in the same way and maintains an unbroken institutional and doctrinal continuity with the Apostolic Church. Those Roman Catholics who object that the Orthodox Church has not held an ecumenical council since 787 and conclude that the Orthodox Church has not pronounced on the great doctrinal issues that have arisen since then, manifest an unawareness of the many local councils held since then, and overestimate the significance of the Roman Catholics' post-787 ecumenical councils, few of which confronted serious doctrinal issues.

Because of all this, I am grateful to God for bringing me back to Holy Orthodoxy. I have had the wondrous privilege of arriving back where I started and knowing the place for the first time. As for my Roman Catholic and Melkite Greek Catholic friends who have professed worry for my soul, I can say that I'm worried about it, too, but not for the reasons they are. If my sinful soul is to be saved, it will be because of the mercy of God I have received in His Holy Orthodox Church.

I am not worried about their souls for doing what they believe in conscience to be the right thing, but my hope and prayer for my Roman Catholic friends is that they, and all Roman Catholics, will explore their church's history and recover an understanding of what the Church was, and what the papacy was, before the Great Schism of 1054. Just as the Church dropped what it regarded as the error of Pope Celestine III from the code of canon law, so now it could renounce the doctrines of ordinary and universal papal jurisdiction and infallibility, for exactly the same reason: they conform neither to Scripture nor to the faith as delineated by the highest authorities of the early and undivided Church.

Once Roman Catholics definitively renounce doctrines that, as I have shown here, it never held, in the first thousand years of the Church anyway, communion between Orthodox and Roman Catholics could be restored, which would be an unimaginable boon for the Church and for the world.

Inconceivable? Maybe. But these are perilous times, and perilous times call for men of faith and courage. Orthodox, Roman Catholics, and Protestants face challenges from various forces arrayed against them as menacing and deadly as any they have faced throughout the history of the Church. Europe, the birthplace of Roman Catholicism, has grown tired of Christianity, and as nature abhors a vacuum, numerous sinister forces have taken advantage of its expulsion. Orthodox Christians all over the Middle East and its environs have suffered oppression for centuries, an oppression that flared up again with new viciousness in the opening decades of the twenty-first century. Nowhere do Christians live in the world today that they aren't assailed by the siren songs of secularism and materialism, and/or beset by the rapacity of persecutors.

It is time to come together. And what better platform could there be upon which to come together than the faith that was held in common, East and West, for the first thousand years of the Church?

UNCUT MOUNTAIN PRESS TITLES

Books by Archpriest Peter Heers

Fr. Peter Heers, *The Ecclesiological Renovation of Vatican II: An Orthodox Examination of Rome's Ecumenical Theology Regarding Baptism and the Church*, 2015

Fr. Peter Heers, *The Missionary Origins of Modern Ecumenism: Milestones Leading up to 1920*, 2007

The Works of our Father Among the Saints, Nikodemos the Hagiorite

Vol. 1: *Exomologetarion: A Manual of Confession*
Vol. 2: *Concerning Frequent Communion of the Immaculate Mysteries of Christ*
Vol. 3: *Confession of Faith*

Other Available Titles

Elder Cleopa of Romania, *The Truth of our Faith, Vol. I: Discourses from Holy Scripture on the Tenants of Christian Orthodoxy.*

Elder Cleopa of Romania, *The Truth of our Faith, Vol. II: Discourses from Holy Scripture on the Holy Mysteries*

Fr. John Romanides, *Patristic Theology: The University Lectures of Fr. John Romanides*

Archimandrite Ephraim Triandaphillopoulos, *Noetic Prayer as the Basis of Mission and the Struggle Against Heresy*

G.M. Davis, *Antichrist: The Fulfillment of Globalization - The Ancient Church and the End of History*

Select Forthcoming Titles

St. Gregory Palamas, *Apodictic Treatise on the Procession of the Holy Spirit*

The Lives and Witness of 20th Century Athonite Fathers

Protopresbyter Anastasios Gotsopoulos, *On Common Prayer with the Heterodox, According to the Canons of the Church*

St. Hilarion Troitsky, *An Overview of the History of the Dogma Concerning the Church*

Elder George of Grigoriou, *Catholicism*

Let No One Fear Death - Collection of essays from Orthodox leaders reflecting on Covidism

Nicholas Baldimtsis, *Life and Witness of St. Iakovos of Evia*

Georgio Kassir, *Errors of the Latins*

This 1st Edition of

THE CHURCH AND THE POPE

written by Robert Spencer and cover design by Michael Jackson, typeset in Baskerville Old Face and Baskerville Italics, and printed through HolyOrthodoxBooks.com in this two thousandth and twenty second year of our Lord's Holy Incarnation, is one of the many fine titles available from Uncut Mountain Press, translators and publishers of Orthodox Christian theological and spiritual literature. Find the book you are looking for at

www.uncutmountainpress.com

GLORY BE TO GOD
FOR ALL THINGS

AMEN.

Made in United States
Orlando, FL
03 September 2024

51087503R00065